BHIKSHUGITA

भिक्षुगीतम्

BHIKSHUGITA

THE MENDICANT'S SONG

(The Story of a Converted Miser)

A Translation
of the 23rd Chapter of the Eknathi Bhagavata

By
JUSTIN E. ABBOTT

Samata Books
Madras

First Published by
Dr. Justin E. Abbott–1928
Samata Edition 1989

10, [illegible] 6, India.

Pr[illegible] 605 001.

CONTENTS

India and the World ... vi

Introduction ... x

Preface to the First Edition ... xi

Song of the Mendicant from Bhagavatam
Translated by Swami Tapasyananda ... xxi

Translation of the Bhikshugita, The Mendicant's Song ... 1

INDIA AND THE WORLD

The literary history of India of the nineteenth century is fascinating with scholars from America, England, France, Italy and other countries visiting our country and becoming eminent scholars of our languages, Sanskrit, Marathi, Bengali, Hindi, Tamil, Telugu, Malayalam, Kannada and the rest. Their advent was of historic interest, and Indian languages and culture benefited remarkably as a result.

Reverend Justin E. Abbott belongs to this magnificent galaxy of scholars. He was born in America in the town of Portsmuth in Hampshire in 1853, and he passed away on June 19, 1932. He was four years old when his parents visited Rahunni in Ahmednagar District of Maharashtra. Years later he came to India as a member of the American Marathi Mission. A scholar and preacher of the literature of the Saints of Maharashtra, Abbott lived in India with his wife for forty years. He was the editor of JNANODAYA, the English section of the American Missions' Journal, for 25 years. He retired from the Mission in 1910 and settled at Summitt in New Jersey, studying the life and writings of the Marathi saints.

Abbott returned to India ten years later in 1920 accompanied by his wife, on a pilgrimage to places revered by the Marathi saints. He spent a month in Pune at the Bharat Itihas Samshodhak Mandal engaged in research, studying the manuscripts of the saints. Later he visited with his wife Daulatabad and other places, particularly the hallowed places where Eknath and his Guru Janardana Swamy lived. Mrs. Abbott was presently taken ill, and she expired at the Miraj Hospital on June 26, 1921. Abbott returned to America thereafter and attended to the work of the American Oriental Society. He visited various Universities in Europe, looking for further information on the literature of the Marathi saints about whom he had already a rich treasure. Besides, he collected valuable information on Shivaji from the correspondence found in the voluminous "Das Register" belonging to the Dutch East India Company. He passed on the material that he gathered to the Bharat Itihas Samshodhak Mandal. His essay on the coins of Shivaji, published by the Asiatic Society, reveals his high regard for the history of Maharashtra.

Abbott wrote a series of articles in JNANODAYA in 1920. Mrs. Abbott was equally fascinated by the literature of the Marathi Saints, which her husband decided to translate into English for the benefit of readers not knowing Marathi. This great work came to be known as "Poet-Saints of Maharashtra" published in a series of volumes. He was hesitant at first to undertake the work, but he was persuaded by his wife and Rev. Edwards of the Theological College of Western India, Pune. Abbott appointed the Marathi Pandit N.R. Godbole to assist him in this task of translation. The actual publication of the work rested with Rev. Edwards who saw it through. This great work on the Poet-Saints of Maharashtra, undertaken and completed by Abbott, placed the people of Maharashtra and India under a deep debt of gratitude to him.

"The Poet-Saints of Maharashtra" consisted of twelve volumes: 1. Bhanudas, 2. Eknath, 3. Bhikshugita, 4. Dasopant Digambar, 5. Bahinabai, 6. Stotramala, 7. Tukaram, 8. Ramdas, 9. Bhaktavijay Vol.I, 10. Bhaktavajay Vol.II, 11. Bhaktaleelamrit, 12. Jnaneshwar.

These volumes contain Abbott's English translation with notes, life-sketches, glossaries and the English meaning of certain Marathi words, besides the Marathi text, Abbott was acquainted with the literature of the Saints of Maharashtra but he did not realise the importance of the Marathi language until he was back in India, and studied the literature once again and came to the conclusion that this body of writing contained the literature of the highest order and supreme message. Abbott desired the welfare of all and wished that every human being should be lifted high exemplifying the essence of real Dharma. Nor did he ever lose his faith in Christ and Christianity.

He was of the opinion that Westerners never understood the Hindu way of Bhakti. He was sorry that he did not realise earlier the Hindu philosophy. He realised that the Hindus had faith in the supreme God though they might worship various idols.

Abbott's love for Maharashtra is evident from his Will in which he left $3,75,000 for Charities, out of which $1,40,000 was set apart for institutions in Maharashtra. The Bharat Itihas Samshodhak Mandal benefited most. Other beneficiaries were:

1. Servants of India Society, Pune.
2. American Mission Hospital, Wai.
3. American Oriental Society.
4. Lepers Sanatorium, France.
5. Gokhale Hall Library, Pune.
6. Social Service League, Bombay.
7. Anath Balikashram, Pune.
8. Depressed Classes Mission, Mangalore.
9. American Lepers Mission.
10. Y.W.C.A. Summitt, USA.
11. Y.M.C.A. Summitt, USA.
12. Overlook Hospital, Summitt, USA.

13. Sevasadan Society, Pune.
14. Rev. Edwards for Poet saints series.
15. American Marathi Mission Naghade Bombay.

The greatness of Abbott and his dedicated service are evident from the foregoing information obtained mostly from the late D.V. Potdar's Arvachina Charitra Kosa.

INTRODUCTION

Samata Books has published already two works of Saint Jnaneshwar: Bhavartha Dipika Jnaneshwari or the Commentary on the Bhagavad Gita as also another work Amritanubhava or Anubhavamrita—both of them translated into English by the late Sri R.K. Bhagwat. It is a pleasure to publish the Works of Saint Eknath translated by Mr. Justin E. Abbott into English from Marathi.

There is a remarkable Gita known as Bhikshugita in 62 slokas in the 23rd chapter of the 11th Section of Srimad Bhagavatam in which Sri Krishna instructs Uddhava on the Spiritual life citing the example of a rich man who was miserly and yet took to the spiritual life later, becoming a beggar suffering much at the hands of persons illtreating him and yet retaining his equanimity and poise which were absent in him in his earlier life. This Gita deals with life as a whole, the rich and the poor, the wise and the foolish, the peaceful and the violent. Saint Eknath has dealt with the Bhikshu Gita from all aspects and in 1004 ovis or verses gave his teaching or Upadesa. His commentary on the Bhikshu Gita is bringing about an inner psychic in the reader or listener.

This volume begins with the Sanskrit text of Bhikshugita followed by its English translation by Swami Tapasyananda of the Ramakrishna Order to enable the reader understand the theme in Srimad Bhagavata and then study the commentary thereon by Saint Eknath.

PREFACE.

While it has been my intention to confine my translations to the accounts of the lives of the Maratha Poet-Saints, that intention is sufficiently flexible to make possible the translation of some of their works, if by doing so I am able to throw light on the character or genius of their pious authors.

I consider Eknāth's version of the Bhikshugita as coming under this head. In expanding the sixty-two verses of the Sanskrit text, into 1004 verses in his Marathi version, he had ample opportunity to express his own thoughts. Thus light is thrown on his own character, as well as on his view point of the ideals of human life.

While the persecutions suffered by the mendicant in the story, represent an extreme case, the persecutions that Eknāth himself had to suffer, because of his consistency to his high principles, were not very unlike those of the converted miser. Eknāth bore his persecutions in the same spirit of humility, of forgiveness, of extraordinary gentleness and self-forgetfulness, as he pictures the trials through which the converted miser had to pass.

The philosophizing of the mendicant on the evil of avarice, on the control of the mind [*mana*], on the philosophy of life, and on the *Bhakti-mārga* [Way of devotion], with its essential of love of God, reflect, I believe, Eknāth's own opinions and the experiences of his own life.

Indian psychology, and terms expressing it, are different from those of the West. This makes an accurate translation very difficult, and a clear understanding of it not at all easy. The Western reader must, therefore, bear this in mind, and not condemn too hastily what may seem to him unreasonable, lest that condemnation be a reflection on his own imperfect knowledge of Indian thought, gained through imperfect translations and inadequate English expressions and words.

While Western readers may differ from the philosophy developed in the Song of the Mendicant, no one can read it without feeling an inspiration for higher living, and for a nobler effort to reach the ideals of life. Eknāth's wish that the reading of his version of the Bhikshugita might bring peace to those troubled by the turmoils of this worldly life, is sure to be realized in some degree by every reader, be he of the East or the West, because of its spirit, breathing the very peace it teaches.

Eknāth's version of the Eleventh *skandha* of the Bhāgavata Purāṇa has great popularity in the Maratha country. There are many old manuscripts of this work. Of printed editions there are four that are available.

Pāngārkar's Eknāthi Bhāgavata. Nirṇayasāgar Press 1915. Difficult words and expressions are explained in footnotes.

Athlye's Eknāthi Bhāgavata, Bombay 1926, with a modern Marathi translation.

Madhavrao's Eknāthi Bhāgavata.

Auti's Eknāthi Bhāgavata, with a modern Marathi translation.

These four editions represent texts that vary slightly in their readings. The correctness of a translation of these texts would have to be judged by the special text it followed.

To the critics of my own translation of the Bhikshugita, I have to ask them to remember that I have used Pāngārkar's text, which differs in some points from other texts. I have to acknowledge difficulty in understanding Eknāth's Marathi of three hundred years ago, in many of his words, now obsolete, and his expressions, unusual in modern Marathi. But I am sure my Maratha critics will view my work with a kindly eye, for they have a kindly heart, and will bear in mind the difficulties that have confronted me.

Here let me acknowledge my indebtedness to Pandit Narhar R. Godbole, for his great assistance in reviewing the first draft of my manuscript and making corrections and suggestions, that will lessen the field of my critics.

The Appendix, containing the text of the Bhikshugita, follows the text of Pāngārkar's edition. Seeing this text through the Press, and preparing the glossary of difficult Marathi words, found in the Bhikshugita, is also the work of Pandit Narhar R. Godbole of Poona.

In issuing this third volume of the Poet-Saints of Mahārāshṭra Series, I wish to express my appreciation of the kindly way in which the preceding two volumes have been received. The present volume is a new venture in a field no translator has thus far entered, and I have reason to believe that it will come as a surprise to many, who are unacquainted with the varying types of Marathi literature.

The volumes in the Poet-Saints of Mahārāshṭra Series, thus far issued are :—

No. 1. Bhānudās, the Great Grandfather of Eknāth.

No. 2. Eknāth, one of the greatest of the Maratha Poet-Saints.

No. 3. Bhikshugita. [The Mendicant's Song]. The twenty-third chapter in Eknāth's version of the eleventh *skandha* of the Bhāgavata Purāṇa.

No. 4. In Press, and soon to be issued, Dāsopant Digambara, a saint contemporary with Eknāth.

No. 5. In course of preparation, Bahiṇābāi, consisting of a translation of her most interesting auto-biography, a poetess contemporary with Tukārām.

No. 6 and following, will be translations of the earliest accounts of the lives of Tukārām, Rāmdās and others.

Perhaps a word of explanation is needed as to why I have used so many Marathi words, making a Glossary necessary. Many words in Sanskrit and Marathi have no exact equivalents in English. It has seemed to me that rather than to mistranslate, it would be better that English readers should learn a few more Indian words, and so enrich their knowledge, while enabling me to keep my translation more exact.

Again I wish to express my thanks to Dr. Nicol Macnicol for his generosity in giving his valuable time to seeing this volume through the Press. Translating in America, and publishing in India, is a task with too many difficulties, were it not for his friendly help.

JUSTIN E. ABBOTT.

SUMMIT, NEW JERSEY, U.S.A.
June 1927.

CONTENTS.

PAGE.

Translation of the Bhikśhugita, The Mendicant's Song 1—1004. ... 1

Preface, Verses 1—76 ... 1

Invocation Verses 1—17 ... 1

Shuka tells Parikshiti of Krishṇa's relating the Bhikshugita to Uddhava. 18—24 ... 3

Contents of Chapters 23—26. 25—29. ... 4

Shuka awakens king Parikshiti's attention 30—46. ... 4

Krishṇa and Uddhava converse on Shānti [Peace of Mind] 47—64. ... 6

The Bhikshugita (Song of the Mendicant) praised. 65—76. ... 8

The Miser of Avanti. 77—102. ... 10

Family and friends turn against the miser. 103—109. ... 12

Ghost-protected wealth. 110—113. ... 13

The Five sacrificial acts. 114—116. 14

The Five partners of wealth. 117—124. ... 14

The miser loses his wealth. 125—136. ... 15

The miser's bodily appearance changes. 137—139. ... 16

The miser becomes a despised man. 140—146. ... 17

The miser repents. 147—163. ... 18

The miser's self-condemnation. 164—174. ... 19

	PAGE.
The converted miser denounces avarice. 175—179. ...	21
The converted miser illustrates the evil of avarice. 180—191	21
Wealth brings anxieties. 192—201. ...	23
Fifteen great evils from love of riches. 202—204.	24
Theft, the first evil from love of riches. 205—212. ...	25
Murder, the second evil from love of riches. 213—219. ...	26
Untruth, the third evil from love of riches. 219—229. ...	26
Hypocrisy, the fourth evil from love of riches. 229—246. ...	28
Sensuality, the fifth evil of love of riches. 247—251. ...	30
Anger, the sixth evil from love of riches. 251—256. ...	30
Pride, the seventh evil from the love of riches. 256—268.	31
Arrogance, the eighth evil from the love of riches. 268—282. ...	32
Disunion, the ninth evil from the love of riches. 282—289. ...	34
Enmity, the tenth evil from the love of riches. 289—299. ...	35
Distrust, the eleventh evil from the love of riches. 299—325.	36
Rivalry, the twelfth evil from the love of riches. 326—331.	38

PAGE.

Immorality, Gambling, Drinking, the thirteenth, fourteenth, and fifteenth evils from the love of riches. 332—344. ... 39

A Bhakta should avoid riches. 345—350. ... 40

Love of riches, a cause of divisions. 351—357. ... 41

Lust for riches makes the noblest birth a failure. 357—364. ... 42

Advantage of a Brahman birth. 365—369. ... 42

Love of riches destroys the Brahman's advantage. 370—374. ... 43

The five great sacrifices of wealth. 375—377. ... 44

The sacrifice of wealth to God. 377. ... 44

The sacrifice of wealth to ancestral spirits. 378 ... 44

The sacrifice of wealth to living parents. 379—384. ... 44

The sacrifice of wealth to Brahmans. 384—387. ... 45

The sacrifice of wealth to mankind. 388—410 ... 46

The confession of the repentant miser. 411—418. ... 48

The repentant miser reflects on the seductions of wealth. 419—423. ... 49

No true enjoyment in mere riches. 424—435. ... 49

The repentant miser regards his loss of wealth as a blessing. 436—446. ... 51

Loss of wealth a sign of God's mercy. 447—455. ... 52

The repentant miser seeks a wholly spiritual life. 456—464. ... 53

The repentant miser prays to God for help. 465—472. ... 54

Krishṇa relates the change in the repentant miser. 473—476. ... 55

PAGE.

The repentant miser decides to become a sannyāsi. 477—487. 56

The repentant miser becomes a true sannyāsi. 488—494. 57

The repentant miser wanders as a sannyāsi. 495—500. ... 58

The repentant miser appears at Avanti as a sannyāsi. 501—502. ... 58

The hostile reception of the sannyāsi 503—505. ... 59

Krishṇa praises the calmness of the sannyāsi. 506—510. ... 59

The sannyāsi is maltreated. 511—515 ... 60

The sannyāsi preserves unruffled calmness. 516—531. ... 60

Insults to make the sannyāsi talk, continue. 532—567. ... 62

The sannyāsi reasons on his sufferings. 568—576. ... 65

The *mana* [mind] is the cause of joy and sorrow. 577—612. ... 66

The sannyāsi explains the characteristics of the *mana*. 613—618. ... 70

How the *mana* is created. 619—633. ... 71

Control of the *mana* is necessary. 634—646. ... 73

Bhakti, as a means for controlling the *mana*. 647—648. ... 74

Means unnecessary if the *mana* is not functioning. 649—663. ... 75

The *mana* dominates the senses. 664—683. 76

The sannyāsi tells of the need of a *guru* to control the *mana*. 684—710. ... 78

PAGE.

The *mana* requires great effort to conquer the *mana*. 711—726. ... 81

The *mana* can conquer the *mana* by friendship. 727—750. ... 83

The *mana* to be treated as enemy or friend. 751—755. 85

The relation of *Ātmā* to the body. 756—771. ... 86

The body not the cause of joy and sorrow to the *Ātmā*. 772—776. ... 88

The *Jiva* does not cause joy or sorrow to the *Ātmā*. 777—782. ... 88

Divinities not the cause of joy or sorrow to the *Ātmā*. 783—800. 89

The *Ātmā* is not the cause of sorrow. 801—814. ... 91

The planets are not the cause of sorrow. 815—834. ... 92

One's *karma* is not the cause of sorrow. 835—848. ... 94

Kāla (Time) is not the cause of sorrow. 848—855. ... 96

Kāla is God and benevolent 856—884. ... 97

The effect of consciousness-of-body. 885—907. ... 99

Right-thinking comes from trust in God. 908—916. ... 102

How one is to approach God. 917—928. ... 103

Krishṇa's praise of the repentant miser. 929—943. ... 104

Krishṇa tells the cause of joy and sorrow. 944—948. ... 106

PAGE.

The conflict between *viveka* and *mana*. 949—961. ... 106

Peace through the control of the *mana*. 962—967. ... 108

The value of the Bhikshugita extolled. 967—979. ... 108

The Song-of-the-Mendicant for the salvation of the world. 980—987. ... 110

Eknāth characterizes his Marathi version of the Bhikshugita. 988—994. ... 111

Eknāth gives the glory to his *Guru*, Janārdan. 995—1004. ... 112

APPENDICES :—

I Glossary of Marathi words used in the Poet-saints of Mahārāshṭra Series. ... 1-28

II Notes on the Bhikshugita ... 1

A. Original Sources of Information regarding Eknāth ... 1

B. The Life of Eknāth, a resumé of Bhaktalilāmṛita Chap. 13—24. ... 2

C. The Bhikshugita 13

1. The Bhāgavata Purāṇa ... 13

2. The Bhikshugita of the Bhāgvata Purāṇa ... 13

3. The Bhikshugita of Eknāth ... 14

SONG OF THE MENDICANT

बादरायणिरुवाच

स एवमाशंसित उद्धवेन भागवतमुख्येन दाशार्हमुख्यः।
सभाजयन् भृत्यवचो मुकुन्दस्तमाबभाषे श्रवणीयवीर्यः ॥ 1॥

The Brahmana of Avanti (1-12)

Sri Suka said: Requested in this way by His great devotee and servant Uddhava, the worshipful Lord who was born as the chief of the Yadus, and whose powers and achievements provide the best material for the human ears to hear, spoke to His servant as follows, expressing His approval of the question. 1

श्रीभगवानुवाच

बार्हस्पत्य स वै नात्र साधुर्वै दुर्जनेरितैः।
दुरुक्तैर्भिन्नमात्मानं यः समाधातुमीश्वरः ॥ 2॥

The worshipful Lord said: O disciple of Brihaspati! There is hardly any one in this world who can control his mind that has been agitated by the evil words of wicked men. 2

न तथा तप्यते विद्धः पुमान् बाणैः सुमर्मगैः।
यथा तुदन्ति मर्मस्था ह्यसतां परुषेषवः ॥ 3॥

The sharp arrows struck at vital parts of the body do not mortify a man to the same extent as the arrows of filthy abuse which evil men release at you. 3

कथयन्ति महत्पुण्यमितिहासमिहोद्धव ।
तमहं वर्णयिष्यामि निबोध सुसमाहितः ॥ 4॥

O Uddhava! Enlightened men have current among them a traditional legend of great holiness in connection with this subject. I shall narrate it to you. Hear it attentively. **4**

केनचिद् भिक्षुणा गीतं परिभूतेन दुर्जनैः ।
स्मरता धृतियुक्तेन विपाकं निजकर्मणाम् ॥ 5॥

Hear this recital of a mendicant who was insulted and ill-treated by some evil men, and who bore it all, taking them to be the result of his own Karma. **5**

अवन्तिषु द्विजः कश्चिदासीदाढ्यतमः श्रिया ।
वार्तावृत्तिः कदर्यस्तु कामी लुब्धोऽतिकोपनः ॥ 6॥

In the country of Avanti there lived a very rich Brahmana holding agriculture and trade as his livelihood. He was highly choleric in temperament, extremely greedy, and very miserly. **6**

ज्ञातयोऽतिथयस्तस्य वाङ्मात्रेणापि नार्चिताः ।
शून्यावसथ आत्मापि काले कामैरनर्चितः ॥ 7॥

He never gave a welcome even verbally to his relatives or guests. In that house empty of inhabitants, there was no proper provision to meet his own needs even. **7**

दुःशीलस्य कदर्यस्य द्रुह्यन्ते पुत्रबान्धवाः ।
दारादुहितरो भृत्या विषण्णा नाचरन् प्रियम् ।। 8।।

His sons and relatives felt oppressed because of his perversity and miserliness. Even his wife, daughters and servants were so depressed that they did not strive to please him. **8**

तस्यैवं यक्षवित्तस्य च्युतस्योभयलोकतः ।
धर्मकामविहीनस्य चुक्रुधुः पञ्चभागिनः ।। 9।।

His five co-sharers' (the agencies adored through Panchamahayajna, namely, Devas, Rishis, Manes, Bhutas and men) were displeased with him, as he never cared to share his wealth with them but only guarded it securely like a goblin (Bhuta). As a consequence, he lost the prospects of his future evolution in the life hereafter and his welfare and enjoyments in this world also. **9**

तदवध्यानविस्रस्तपुण्यस्कन्धस्य भूरिद ।
अर्थोऽप्यगच्छन्निधनं बह्वायासपरिश्रमः ।।10।।

For, the anger of the deities of Panchayajna deprived him even of that merit which had enabled him to accumulate wealth. As a consequence his entire wealth was dissipated in spite of all the hard work he was putting in for its acquisition. **10**

ज्ञातयो जगृहुः किंचित् किंचिद् दस्यव उद्धव ।
दैवतः कालतः किंचिद् ब्रह्मबन्धोर्नृपार्थिवात् ।।11।।

.His relatives appropriated some of it, thieves relieved him of some; and fire, accident, bad seasons, and the exactions of kings completed the process of his impoverishment. **11**

स एवं द्रविणे नष्टे धर्मकामविवर्जितः ।
उपेक्षितश्च स्वजनैश्चिन्तामाप दुरत्ययाम् ॥12॥

Deprived now of the means to perform his religious duties and meet his worldly needs, and deserted also by all his relatives, he came to be filled with worrying thoughts. **12**

तस्यैवं ध्यायतो दीर्घं नष्टरायस्तपस्विनः ।
खिद्यतो बाष्पकण्ठस्य निर्वेदः सुमहानभूत् ॥13॥

He becomes a Mendicant (13-30)

As he was thus being mentally burnt by the sorrow arising from total impoverishment and was shedding bitter tears about his condition over and over again, there arose in him by the Lord's grace a powerful fit of renunciation for all worldly values. **13**

स चाहेदमहो कष्टं वृथाऽऽत्मा मेऽनुतापितः ।
न धर्माय न कामाय यस्यार्थायास ईदृशः ॥14॥

He began to think: 'Vain has been all my hard work for the acquisition of wealth which I failed to use for religious work or worldly enjoyments. **14**

प्रायेणार्थाः कदर्याणां न सुखाय कदाचन ।
इह चात्मोपतापाय मृतस्य नरकाय च ॥15॥

The wealth of misers never turns out to be a means of happiness. Its rewards are worry here and hell hereafter. **15**

यशो यशस्विनां शुद्धं श्लाघ्या ये गुणिनां गुणाः ।
लोभः स्वल्पोऽपि तान् हन्ति श्वित्रो रूपमिवेप्सितम् ।।16।।

Just as leucoderma mars the beauty of even a perfect form, even a little of miserliness compromises the clean reputation and the otherwise praiseworthy character of men. **16**

अर्थस्य साधने सिद्धे उत्कर्षे रक्षणे व्यये ।
नाशोपभोग आयासस्त्रासश्चिन्ता भ्रमो नृणाम् ।।17।।

Great effort is required to earn, augment and protect wealth. Even if it is acquired, in expending and enjoying it, great fear and worry are likely, while its loss will depress man and bring him to the brink of madness. **17**

स्तेयं हिंसानृतं दम्भः कामः क्रोधः स्मयो मदः ।
भेदो वैरमविश्वासः संस्पर्धा व्यसनानि च ।।18।।
एते पञ्चदशानर्था ह्यर्थमूला मता नृणाम् ।
तस्मादनर्थमर्थाख्यं श्रेयोऽर्थी दूरतस्त्यजेत् ।।19।।

Theft, slaughter, falsehood, hypocrisy, greed, anger, egotism, pride, partiality, rancour, suspicion, jealousy, sexuality, gambling, drunkenness—these fifteen vices are produced in men by wealth, according to the view of wise ones. So let those who aspire after liberation abandon it from afar, as *artha*, wealth, is really *anartha*, the cause of all evil. **18-19**

भिद्यन्ते भ्रातरो दाराः पितरः सुहृदस्तथा।
एकास्निग्धाः काकिणिना सद्यः सर्वेऽरयः कृताः ॥20॥

Brothers, wives, parents and such close relatives so dear to one another, and living together as if they were one in body, become bitter enemies for the sake of a few coins. **20**

अर्थेनाल्पीयसा ह्येते संरब्धा दीप्तमन्यवः।
त्यजन्त्याशु स्पृधो घ्नन्ति सहसोत्सृज्य सौहृदम् ॥21॥

Dispute over a trifle is sufficient to inflame them with anger and make them fight among themselves forgetting all loving relationship and ever intent on mutual destruction. **21**

लब्ध्वा जन्माऽमरप्रार्थ्यं मानुषं तद्द्विजाग्र्यताम्।
तदनादृत्य ये स्वार्थं घ्नंति यांत्यशुभां गतिम् ॥22॥

Birth among the most abominable species is the dismal reward for those who, having obtained a human birth and that as a Brahmana—a circumstance which is the highest aspiration even of Devas—, cast it off like a trifle without striving for the attainment of spiritual freedom, which is the highest end of living beings. **22**

स्वर्गापवर्गयोर्द्वारं प्राप्य लोकमिमं पुमान्।
द्रविणे कोऽनुषज्जेत मर्त्योऽनर्थस्य धामनि ॥23॥

A person does not deserve to be called human who fails to make a proper use of this embodiment as man, the gateway to heaven and liberation, but runs after wealth, which is the source of every kind of misery during the short span of life given to him. **23**

देवर्षिपितृभूतानि ज्ञातीन् बन्धूंश्च भागिनः ।
असंविभज्य चात्मानं यक्षवित्तः पतत्यधः ॥24॥

Surely downfall awaits a man who accumulates wealth like a treasure-guarding Yaksha without distributing their shares of it among the deities, Rishis, Pitris, elementals, relatives, associates and others who have claims on it. **24**

व्यर्थयाऽर्थेहया वित्तं प्रमत्तस्य वयो बलम् ।
कुशला येन सिद्धयंति जरठः किं नु साधये ॥25॥

Oblivious of all the higher values of life because of vain greed for wealth, my strength, my life and my wealth too have all gone to sheer waste. Wise men utilise wealth as means to salvation. But what can I, an old and decrepit man, now do? **25**

कस्मात् संक्लिश्यते विद्वान् व्यर्थयार्थेहयासकृत् ।
कस्यचिन्मायया नूनं लोकोऽयं सुविमोहितः ॥26॥

How is it then that even wise men, who know all these evil consequences of the pursuit of wealth, struggle for it without stop in spite of all difficulties? Surely it is because the whole world is under the spell of delusion cast by the Maya of the Lord of infinite potency. **26**

किं धनैर्धनदैर्वा किं कामैर्वा कामदैरुत ।
मृत्युना ग्रस्यमानस्य कर्मभिर्वोत जन्मदैः ॥27॥

For man who is already in the mouth of the serpent of death, of what significance is wealth and those who help him to get it? Of what use are enjoyments too, and those who provide him with them? **27**

नूनं मे भगवांस्तुष्टः सर्वदेवमयो हरिः ।
येन नीतो दशामेतां निर्वेदश्चात्मनः प्लवः ॥28॥

Surely the worshipful Lord, Hari, the embodiment of all divinities, has been pleased with me and brought me to this state of mind. He has provided me out of His grace with this boat of renunciation with which I can cross the ocean of Samsara. **28**

सोऽहं कालावशेषेण शोषयिष्येऽङ्गमात्मनः ।
अप्रमत्तोऽखिलस्वार्थे यदि स्यात् सिद्ध आत्मनि ॥29॥

Whatever length of my life-span is still left for me, I shall dedicate it to the earnest pursuit of the higher values of life, finding my joy exclusively in the Atman, and subjecting my body to rigorous discipline for this purpose. **29**

तत्र मामनुमोदेरन् देवास्त्रिभुवनेश्वराः ।
मुहूर्तेन ब्रह्मलोकं खट्वाङ्गः समसाधयत् ॥30॥

In this effort may I have the blessing of all the Divinities who are the rulers of the three worlds. By the Lord's grace, the King Khatvanga attained to Brahmaloka in a trice. Why not I too?' **30**

श्रीभगवानुवाच

इत्यभिप्रेत्य मनसा ह्यावन्त्यो द्विजसत्तमः ।
उन्मुच्य हृदयग्रन्थीन् शान्तो भिक्षुरभून्मुनिः ॥31॥

Mendicant persecuted (31-42)

The worshipful Lord said: Resolving like this in mind, that Brahmana of Avanti abandoned all the knotty desires of his heart, became tranquil and took to the life of a mendicant. **31**

स चचार महीमेतां संयतात्मेद्रियानिलः ।
भिक्षार्थं नगरग्रामानसंगोऽलक्षितोऽविशत् ॥32॥

With his mind, senses, and Pranas controlled, he wandered from one place to another all over the country, entering towns and villages only for alms, completely unattached, and in no way demonstrating his greatness. **32**

तं वै प्रवयसं भिक्षुमवधूतमसज्जनाः ।
दृष्ट्वा पर्यभवन् भद्र बह्वीभिः परिभूतिभिः ॥33॥

O good friend! Evil men persecuted and insulted him in many ways, seeing him old, decrepit, untended and ill-clad. **33**

केचित्त्रिवेणुं जगृहुरेके पात्रं कमंडलुम् ।
पीठं चैकेऽक्षसूत्रं च कंथां चीराणि केचन ॥34॥

Some pulled at his staff; some at his water pot and begging

bowl; some at his seat; some at his beads; and some at his rags and bark-cloth. **34**

प्रदाय च पुनस्तानि दर्शितान्याददुर्मुनेः।
अन्नं च भैक्ष्यसम्पन्नं भुञ्जानस्य सरित्तटे ॥35॥
मूत्रयन्ति च पापिष्ठाः ष्ठीवन्त्यस्य च मूर्धनि।
यतवाचं वाचयन्ति ताडयन्ति न वक्ति चेत् ॥36॥

Some gave back to him his personal effects, only to take them away again. Some wretches among them passed urine in the mendicant's food collected by holy alms, while he was taking it on the river bank. Some others spat on his head. They tried their best to break his vow of silence; and when they failed, they thrashed him to make him speak. **35-36**

तर्जयन्त्यपरे वाग्भिः स्तेनोऽयमिति वादिनः।
बध्नन्ति रज्ज्वा तं केचिद् बध्यतां बध्यतामिति ॥37॥

Some tried to frighten him shouting that he was a thief, while others proceeded to bind him with cords. **37**

क्षिपन्त्येकेऽवजानन्त एष धर्मध्वजः शठः।
क्षीणवित्त इमां वृत्तिमग्रहीत् स्वजनोज्झितः ॥38॥

Still others insulted him by declaring him a hypocrite, who, having lost all his belongings and being deserted by his friends, had assumed this mendicant's role only to deceive people. **38**

अहो एंष महासारो धृतिमान् गिरिराडिव।
मौनेन साधयत्यर्थं बकवद् दृढनिश्चयः ॥39॥

Some said: 'Possessed of great strength of mind and endurance that will do credit to a mountain, this man remains silent like a crane with determination and achieves his purpose. It is most remarkable indeed!' **39**

इत्येके विहसन्त्येनमेके दुर्वातयन्ति च।
तं बबन्धुर्निरुरुधुर्यथा क्रीडनकं द्विजम् ॥40॥

While some made fun of him like this, others passed dirty wind at him, and still others bound, imprisoned and treated him like a pet animal or bird. **40**

एवं स भौतिकं दुःखं दैविकं दैहिकं च यत्।
भोक्तव्यमात्मनो दिष्टं प्राप्तं प्राप्तमबुध्यत ॥41॥

Whatever sufferings came to him in this manner from external, supernatural, or mental sources, he put up with them all with the thought that he was bound to suffer them all as a part of his Prarabdha. **41**

परिभूत इमां गाथामगायत नराधमैः।
पातयद्भिः स्वधर्मस्थो धृतिमास्थाय सात्त्विकीम् ॥42॥

Though evil men thus tried their best to shake him from his Swadharma by persecutions, he remained steadfast in his Sattvika nature and his Swadharma. He recited the following stanzas: **42**

द्विज उवाच

नायं जनो मे सुखदुःखहेतुर्न देवतात्मा ग्रहकर्मकालाः ।
मनः परं कारणमामनन्ति संसारचक्रं परिवर्तयेद् यत् ॥43॥

Mind as Cause of Samsara (43-50)

The Mendicant said: These men are not the cause of my enjoyments and sufferings; it is neither any divinity, nor the self, nor any star, nor Karma, nor Time. The mind alone is the sole cause for turning this wheel of Samsara, according to the views of great men. **43**

मनो गुणान् वै सृजते बलीयस्ततश्च कर्माणि विलक्षणानि ।
शुक्लानि कृष्णान्यथ लोहितानि तेभ्यः सवर्णाः सृतयो भवन्ति ॥44॥

The powerful mind generates the modes and movements of all the senses. Out of the senses proceed actions which are of the nature of Sattva, Rajas or Tamas. Out of actions, according to their nature, embodiments as celestials, men and brute creations take place. **44**

अनीह आत्मा मनसा समीहता हिरण्मयो मत्सख उद्विचष्टे ।
मनः स्वलिङ्गं परिगृह्य कामान् जुषन् निबद्धो गुणसङ्गतोऽसौ ॥45॥

Though seen in association with the active mind, the Atman (the Jiva's closest friend), who is charged with the power of knowledge, is never an actor but stands out as the witness of the modes of the mind and the actions of the senses. But the Jiva identifies himself with that mind whose activity projects the Samsara on the Atman. Through this imaginative identification, the Jiva appears to be subject to the enjoyments and sufferings that arise from the activities of the mind. **45**

दानं स्वधर्मो नियमो यमश्च श्रुतं च कर्माणि च सद्व्रतानि।
सर्वे मनोनिग्रहलक्षणान्ताः परो हि योगो मनसः समाधिः ॥46॥

Charity, discharge of one's duties, tranquillity of mind and the senses, study of scriptures, various kinds of rituals and vows—all these have control of the mind as their one object. Subjugation of the mind is Samadhi, the establishment of the mind in peace. It is the highest Yoga. **46**

समाहितं यस्य मनः प्रशान्तं दानादिभिः किं वद तस्य कृत्यम्।
असंयतं यस्य मनो विनश्यद् दानादिभिश्चेदपरं किमेभिः ॥47॥

If a man's mind has already attained one-pointedness and tranquillity, of what further use are charity and other disciplines for him? And pray, of what use are charity and other disciplines if his mind continues to run after sense enjoyments or is immersed in torpor and lethargy? **47**

मनोवशेऽन्ये ह्यभवन् स्म देवा मनश्च नान्यस्य वशं समेति।
भीष्मो हि देवः सहसः सहीयान् युञ्ज्याद् वशे तं स हि देवदेवः ॥48॥

All the other senses are subject to the mind, but not the mind to any other. This formidable entity, mind, is more powerful than any other centre of power. He who has been able to conquer it, is the true master of all the senses. **48**

तं दुर्जयं शत्रुमसह्यवेगमरुंतुदं तन्न विजित्य केचित् ।
कुर्वन्त्यसद्विग्रहमत्र मर्त्यैर्मित्राण्युदासीनरिपून् विमूढाः ॥49॥

Without conquering or making an effort to conquer this almost invincible enemy, one's own mind, which works with unimaginable speed and pierces all the vital parts, foolish man enters into vain quarrels with others, looking upon them as friends, enemies or neutrals. **49**

देहं मनोमात्रमिमं गृहीत्वा ममाहमित्यन्धधियो मनुष्याः ।
एषोऽहमन्योऽयमिति भ्रमेण दुरन्तपारे तमसि भ्रमन्ति ॥50॥

Subject to the delusion of taking one's body, which is a product of mental construction, as oneself, men with clouded minds look upon themselves and others as entirely different beings and thus entangle themselves in the darkness of endless Samsara. **50**

जनस्तु हेतुः सुखदुःखयोश्चेत् किमात्मनश्चात्र ह भौमयोस्तत् ।
जिह्वां क्वचित् संदशति स्वदद्भिस्तद्वेदनायां कतमाय कुप्येत् ॥51॥

The Unaffected Atman (51-56)

Supposing for argument's sake it is accepted that it is others that cause your happiness and misery, how does this position in any way affect the Atman who is spirit and not the body? What is done by others to the body cannot affect the Atman. But still if you say that the pain and pleasure caused by others, even if it be to the body, is in some way felt by the Atman, then, since the Atman in yourself and in the enemies is the same, where is the reason for being pleased or annoyed with them? When one's tongue is bitten by one's own teeth, no one gets annoyed with oneself for causing the resulting pain. **51**

दुःखस्य हेतुर्यदि देवतास्तु किमात्मनस्तत्र विकारयोस्तत्।
यदङ्गमङ्गेन निहन्यते क्वचित् क्रुध्येत कस्मै पुरुषः स्वदेहे ॥52॥

If it is said that the agent inflicting suffering and the subject undergoing suffering, are the deities presiding over the limb inflicting suffering and the limb affected by suffering, even then it is of no consequence to the changeless Atman. It is also like one limb of the body striking at another limb—a situation in which it may be asked: Who is to be angry and at whom? For the deities in the limbs of both the persons involved are one and the same. **52**

आत्मा यदि स्यात् सुखदुःखहेतुः किमन्यतस्तत्र निजस्वभावः।
न ह्यात्मनोऽन्यद् यदि तन्मृषा स्यात् क्रुध्येत कस्मान्न सुखं न दुःखम् ॥53॥

If it be the contention that the Atman, in the course of his self-caused evolutionary process, brings on himself happiness and suffering, then at whom can one be angry, as that suffering is natural, being self-caused? If it is said that it is caused by another, then it is answered there is no 'another', the Atman being the sole existence. The 'another' is only an appearance and not a reality. As there is thus no cause outside Atman, there can be neither joy nor sorrow brought about by another. **53**

ग्रहा निमित्तं सुखदुःखयोश्चेत् किमात्मनोऽजस्य जनस्य ते वै।
ग्रहैर्ग्रहस्यैव वदन्ति पीडां क्रुध्येत कस्मै पुरुषस्ततोऽन्यः ॥54॥

If the planets are the cause of happiness and misery, of what consequence is it to the birthless and deathless Atman? The influence of the planets must be confined only to the body that is born in the specific periods of time influenced by them. The masters of astrology say that planets affict only one another by their various positions, postures and influences. What does it matter to the Atman? The bodies born at the times influenced by them may be affected, but it does not touch the Atman. (Even if the bodies are affected, it is only because of identification with particular constellations.) 54

कर्मास्तु हेतुः सुखदुःखयोश्चेत् किमात्मनस्तद्धि जडाजडत्वे ।
देहस्त्वचित् पुरुषोऽयं सुपर्णः क्रुध्येत कस्मै न हि कर्ममूलम् ॥55॥

Some say that Karma is the cause of happiness and misery. But as the Atman is by nature actionless, how can Karma (action and its results) affect him? Besides, Karma can affect only something that is at the same time 'inert and conscious'. It is however inconsistent to say so. The Atman is always conscious and the body is always inert. So there can be nothing that is 'conscious and inert' at the same time. In its absence there can be nothing like Karma too, much less joy and suffering arising from it. 55

कालस्तु हेतुः सुखदुःखयोश्चेत् किमात्मनस्तत्र तदात्मकोऽसौ ।
नाग्नेर्हि तापो न हिमस्य तत स्यात् क्रुध्येत कस्मै न परस्य द्वन्द्वम् ॥56॥

If the cause of enjoyment and suffering is said to be Time, how can it affect the Atman? For this Atman is Time itself. Fire does not burn up tongues of flame, which are only its parts, nor does cold destroy or melt its products like ice pieces?

The Atman is beyond the pairs of opposites like suffering and enjoyment. Whom then will one be angry at? **56**

न केनचित् क्वापि कथंचनास्य द्वन्द्वोपरागः परतः परस्य।
यथाहमः संसृतिरूपिणः स्यादेवं प्रबुद्धो न बिभेति भूतैः ॥57॥

I-sense as the Experiencer of Samsara (57-62)

It is the I-sense, the experiencer of the cycle of births and deaths, that gets attracted to the pairs of opposites like heat and cold, pleasure and pain, virtue and vice etc. To the Atman, supreme over all entities considered the highest in man's relative scale, this attachment to the pairs of opposites can never happen. It is the one who has not awakened to this truth that is subject to fear from others. **57**

एतां स आस्थाय परात्मनिष्ठामध्यासितां पूर्वतमैर्महर्षिभिः।
अहं तरिष्यामि दुरन्तपारं तमो मुकुन्दाङ्घ्रिनिषेवयैव ॥58॥

Adopting this discipline of subsidence in the Supreme Self following the example of great Rishis of the past, and taking to the service of the feet of the worshipful Mukunda, I shall soon bet across the limitless expanse of the darkness of ignorance. **58**

श्रीभगवानुवाच

निर्विद्य नष्टद्रविणो गतक्लमः प्रव्रज्य गां पर्यटमान इत्थम्।
निराकृतोऽसद्भिरपि स्वधर्मादकम्पितोऽमुं मुनिराह गाथाम् ॥59॥

The worshipful Lord said: Thus did that mendicant proclaim, on losing all his wealth and thereby attaining complete dispassion and freedom from all worldly cares. Though insulted and persecuted by evil men, he roamed over the land without budging even an inch from his characteristic ways of life (Swadharma) in the face of all these provocations and difficulties. **59**

सुखदुःखप्रदो नान्यः पुरुषस्यात्मविभ्रमः ।
मित्रोदासीनरिपवः संसारस्तमसः कृतः ॥60॥

This Samsara, producing happiness and misery and the distinction of friend, foe and neutral, is a delusion of the mind; it is entirely a product of ignorance. (Sufferings and enjoyments spring from this state itself, not from any outside factor.) **60**

तस्मात् सर्वात्मना तात निगृहाण मनो धिया ।
मय्यावेशितया युक्त एतावान् योगसंग्रहः ॥61॥

O Uddhava! Therefore, equipped with a mind that is entirely dedicated to Me, put in your best effort to control the mind. This is the sum and substance of all Yoga. **61**

य एतां भिक्षुणा गीतां ब्रह्मनिष्ठां समाहितः ।
धारयञ्छ्रावयञ्छृण्वन् द्वन्द्वैर्नैवाभिभूयते ॥62॥

इति श्रीमद्भागवते महापुराणे पारमहंस्यां संहितायामेकादशस्कन्धे
त्रयोविंशोऽध्यायः ॥23॥

Whoever hears with faith and devotion this song of the medicant dealing with the subject of establishment in Brahmic consciousness or makes others hear it and themselves constantly think over it will not be overcome by the contradictions of life. **62**

BHIKSHUGITA, THE MENDICANT'S SONG

(THE STORY OF A CONVERTED MISER)

A commentary by Eknāth on the 23rd chapter of the Eleventh *Skandha* of the Bhāgavata Purāṇa.

PREFACE, VERSES 1 TO 76

Invocation

OBEISANCE TO ŚRI GAṆEŚA

1. Obeisance to Thee, O Sadguru, [a](Thou who appearest in) the form of the Universe; Thou who art in and without the Universe in Thy essential form of Intelligence. Yet, though thus attributing to Thee that form, Thou art formless and without parts. 2. The variety in which the animate and inanimate appears is but the variations in Thy formlessness. *Jiva* [b][individual *ātmā*] and *Shiva* [universal *ātmā*] are but Thy *Māyā*. Non-duality is Thy glory. 3. A statue, made of solid *ghi*, appears as a form, but from the point of view of the *ghi* itself, it is formless. So Thou, who art without parts, and indestructible appearest in the form of the Universe. 4. The Universe, which appears in a definite form, is in reality Thy body. But though viewed as Thy body, Thou art, however, bodiless; and yet even bodilessness is not to be ascribed to Thee. 5. Thou art not what appears to be, and yet Thou art what is not. Still there is no such thing with Thee as becoming or not-becoming. Such art Thou, the Universal *guru* of this Universe. 6. The (idea of) sound

---

a. In ( ) completion of meaning. *b.* In [ ] explanation.

is one remote from Thee, and yet Thou art within and without sound. Thou art He who speaks in all animate and inanimate creation. Thou art the Speaker in the *Vedas* and *shāstras.* 7. Sweetness is obtained from the sugar-cane. The sugar-cane has sweetness within and without it, but there is no sugar-cane in the sweetness. In that same good sense Thou art related to the *Vedas.* 8. Thou alone art the Speaker in the *Vedas,* and it is in the *Vedas* that Thou art described. And yet in the final analysis Thou art incomprehensible even by the *Vedas.* Thou, O *Guru* dear, dwellest where words cannot describe. 9. Just as sound in the abstract is inaudible until something is struck; and as there is no musical instrument that can make this inaudible sound, 10, so Thou art the Speaker in the *Vedas,* and the inspirer of all *shāstras,* and yet accepted as Thou art by the whole *Vedas* and *Shāstras* they cannot in truth describe Thee. 11. If then one should assert that Thou art indescribable, this discussion of Thy being indescribable or describable arises from Thy *Māyā.* Thou art not to be known in that way.

12. Thou alone art the knower of the fact that Thou art unknowable. But in asserting the fact that Thou art the knower, the idea of Thy unknowableness disappears. 13. Where there is lacking the idea of not knowing, how can there be the idea of knowing? If there exists no such idea as a wife, who would say "Look at her husband " 14. Thou art, therefore, neither a Knower nor a Not-knower. Thou art neither a Speaker nor a Non-speaker. Thou art not Many, nor One. Thy very incomprehensibleness is incomprehensible. 15. Thou art indescribable in words, formless, qualitiless, and without self-consciousness. But in thus defining Thee, one is lost in a dilemma, for Thou

hast the form of the Universe, and art the Soul of the Universe. 16. It is evident Thou art in the form of the Universe, and being so, whose duality can injure whom? There is no other (than Thyself). Then who is there to feel the intense antagonistic wrongs of another (than Thyself)? 17. Thus O *Sadguru,* my Lord, at Thy feet Duality becomes Oneness, and in accordance with that Oneness Thou art continuing in the Śri Bhāgavata the story of Thyself.

SHUKA TELLS PARIKSHITI OF KRISHṆA'S RELATING THE BHIKSHUGITA TO UDDHAVA

18. In the Śri Bhāgavata, at the close of the 22nd chapter, Uddhava is declared to have asked (Krishṇa) regarding Peace-of-mind [*shānti*] and the means for ending Duality. 19. Uddhava had asked a very wide question, in receving an answer to which his desire for the knowledge of Brahma was satisfied. The question was pleasing to Śuka, and in relating it he satisfied the wish of Parikshiti. 20. Hearing the question put by Uddhava, Śuka was deeply moved with feelings of joy, and exclaimed "O Parikshiti, give close attention. Shripati [Krishṇa] is pleased with Uddhava 21. The state of *Nirvāṇ,* which comes from the Knowledge-of-Brahma, is the special form of Peace-of-Mind [*shānti*]. It was regarding this special *Shānti* that Uddhava raised the question in love and Shripati [Krishṇa] was pleased with it.

22. In the four succeeding chapters Krishṇa is about to describe *Śhānti* and *Nivritti,* so listen, O King Parikshiti, while I relate to you what Krishṇa is to say. 23. Listen, O Light-of-the-Pāndava-family, O chief-of-the-Kaurava-family. You have rightly the authority to possess this

Peace, because you are a seeker after peace-of-soul. 24. In order to acquire the knowledge-of-Brahma you have ceased even to drink water, that you might listen, therefore, listen O King, to what Hari [Krishṇa] is about to relate of *Shānti* and *Nivritti.*"

CONTENTS OF CHAPTERS 23 to 26

25. In this 23rd chapter there is the description of one whose mind [*mana*] evil men attempted to ruffle, but to his *mana* there came full forgiveness. It is his story that Śri Krishṇa is about to relate in this 23rd character. 26. This Bhikshugita has for its special subject the control of the *mana* [mind]. The subject of the control of Prakriti [one's individual self] will be fully developed in the 24th chapter. 27. After describing the three *guṇas* [the qualities] Krishṇa caused Uddhava's attention to His own *nirguṇ* [without qualities] state. In the 25th chapter the control of the *guṇas* is clearly explained. 28. The 26th chapter contains the subject of absolute freedom from worldly desires. After this follows the Ailagita, which teaches the rejection of every object of sense, women and all else. 29. In these four chapters respectively, Krishṇa, with his own lips, clearly explains the control of the *mana* [mind], Prakriti [one's individual self], objects of sense, and the *guṇas* [the qualities].

ŚRI ŚUKA AWAKENS KING PARIKSHITI'S ATTENTION.

30. It was in the following words that Śri Śuka, the great *yogi,* made Parikshiti attentive, and put before him the contents of the story (of the miser).

31. Śuka said, "O Parikshiti, Shripati [Krishṇ] was pleased with the sentiments he heard Uddhava utter, and expressed himself thus to Uddhava. 32. "Only at the end of ten millions of years does one acquire Brahmanhood in a noble family. Such a birth is the natural fruit of supreme good deeds. But it is fruitless, if it is without devotion [*bhakti*] to Hari. 33. There may exist a fruitful mango tree, but overgrown with a parasite. Though by nature it is a fruitful tree, you perceive that it becomes unfruitful. Such is the case with even good people who lack devotion to God.

34. Such is not the case with Uddhava. He has had a noble birth in the Yādava family line. Even if he has reached the highest social position, he has not been seduced by prosperity. 35. O Mahārāj! He who, though possessed with royal riches, does not neglect the worship [*bhakti*] of God, acquires of a certainty the chief place among God's worshippers. 36. He who will not neglect the path of God, even for a noble, beautiful, dutiful, and lovely wife, bears the name of being God's special *bhakta.* 37. Uddhava possesses these characteristics in a high degree. Through right-thinking [*viveka*] he has entirely lost his desire for worldly things, and chief among the worshippers of God, is attached to the feet of Śri Krishṇa. 38. The greatness that comes merely from age or wealth, is utter inferiority. True greatness is in acquiring God, and through the blessing that comes from it, Uddhava became perfect. 39. He was the trusted one of Śri Krishṇa. Śri Krishṇa used to take him privately aside, and give him the mystic knowledge. How can I sufficiently praise his good fortune!

40. The Supreme-Brahma, manifested as Krishṇa, was at Udhava's command, and because he followed His teachings, he was the one especially blessed in his good fortune." 41. As Śuka continued to relate the happy fortune of Uddhava, he was choked with emotion; he overflowed with joy, and became speechless through the superabundance of his happiness. 42. When the chief of the Kauravas [King Parikshiti] saw that in relating this extreme good fortune of Uddhava, Śri Śuka was overcome with emotion, he became intensely astonished. 43. In relating the happy fortune of Uddhava Śri Śuka was overcome with emotion, and I also acknowledge Uddhava's good fortune. 44. Śuka then said to the king [Parikshiti], "Because Uddhava was possessed with supreme good fortune, when he made his request to Hrishikeśi [Krishṇa], he was greatly pleased with his question. 45. Uddhava had a longing for Peace of mind [*shānti*] and Uddhava's question regarding it was pleasing to Śri Krishṇa. To satisfy, therefore, Uddhava's desire, Krishṇa tells a story at length. 46. "You are certainly one with authority to acquire supreme Peace of mind" said Krishṇa, and then making of his love for Uddhava an opportunity, Śri Hari [Krishṇa] then explained that Peace of mind [*shānti*].

KRISHṆA AND UDDHAVA CONVERSE ON SHĀNTI [PEACE-OF-MIND].

47. "Uddhava, what you have asserted, I accept as true. No ordinary man possesses so peaceful a mind as to be able to bear the insults of evil men. 48. He to whose *pādukās* [foot-prints] the gods bow with their heads; He at whose

feet the great Indra falls; He to whom the great *Siddhis* [mystic powers] are slaves; He at whose bidding stands the Knowledge-of-Brahma; 49. He, namely Brihaspati, the *guru* of the gods,—you are his disciple. You are Right-thinking [*viveka*] in visible form. Therefore you certainly may learn the way to acquire that Peace-of-mind."

50. But that Uddhava might grasp the full meaning of *shānti* [peace-of-mind], Hrishikeśi [Krishṇa] politely accepted his statement, and assented to his assertion, and then proceeded to describe what pure *shānti* is. 51. "When evil men insult, he who can endure their insults, contempt and scorn, is himself God, perfect in his enlightenment, one in form with me. 52. He who is deeply pervaded with the thought that he himself is in all creatures, such an one willingly bears the blows of evil men. 53. He who sees himself as the whole universe, though he be afflicted by many troubles, he has no rise of angry feelings within him. He willingly bears troubles without pain. 54. If one's own hand slaps one's own body no exclamation of anger or hatred is provoked. So he who sees himself as the animate and inanimate, *Shānti* [Peace of Mind] enters his abode of her own accord. 55. Uddhava, He, who is thus enlightened, is called a true *Sādhu* [saint]. He bears the wrongs done him by others. He is a true example of one possessing pure peace-of-mind.

56. Those wise men, whose knowledge does not include this knowledge of themselves, they cannot bear the sufferings that arise from Duality. Listen! I will explain. 57. The word-arrows of evil men cause deeper wounds than even do the sharpest of steel arrows, whose piercings cause one to writhe in agony. 58. Wherever a steel

tipped arrow pierces there is local pain, but the power of word-arrows is greater. It even wounds one's ancestors. 59. If one is wounded by the piercing of a steel-tipped arrow, the pain can be cured by a leaf-poultice, but if pierced by a word-arrow the sore remains for life. 60. When the word-arrows of insult, with their poison that reaches the very vitals, pierce one, they lacerate the heart, and the whole body is set afflame. 61. It is therefore certainly true that the ordinary man has not the *shānti* [peace of mind] necessary for bearing the evil words of men, and their impertinent insults."

62. Thus mindful of the thought of Uddhava, Śri Krishṇa begins the attempt to illustrate (by a story) the true meaning of *shānti* [peace of mind], 63. He said to Uddhava "Hasten to acquire the peace-of-mind already described." He thought of the difficulties Uddhava would feel, and the disappointments he would meet, 64. For it was in Uddhava's thought that *Shānti* was impossible for all men to attain. Knowing this Hrishikeśi [Krishṇa] related the story called the Bhikshugita [Song of the Mendicant].

THE BHIKSHUGITA [SONG OF THE MENDICANT] PRAISED.

65. These supremely pure words of Krishṇa, a veritable Gaṅgā, in the form of a historical tale, are for the purpose of immediately washing away the filth of the heart, consisting of passions and unrest. 66 This Peace-Godavari river has its birth beneath the Audumbar tree, namely the Shri Bhagavata, on Mount Brahma, namely the mouth of Shri Krishṇa. Thus from its very source it is pure. 67. Then passing by a subterranian passage, Naradlike, it

suddenly appears, at Gaṅgādvāra in the form of Uddhava, through the words of Vyāsa. Then again the same river, through the mouth of Shuka appears suddenly at Kushavarta in its purifying power. 68. The course of this holy stream eastward is formed from the union of the rivers Aruṇā, Varuṇā and Sarasvati, namely Faith, Courage and *Bhakti.* 69. Into the high overflowing flood of this Peace-Gaṅga-River those keen to listen take their plunge and become holy through their forgiving spirit.

70. Śri Krishṇa revealed this far-famed Peace-Gaṅgā-river in relating the Mendicant's Song [Bhikshugita] for the purpose of making Uddhava holy.

71. "Uddhava", said Krishṇa "a certain *sannyāsi,* when being troubled by some evil-minded persons, said to himself, "My evil deeds are being destroyed (through their persecution)." And thus this forgiving man became happy. 72. When one's filth is being washed away through others, he who lets anger disturb his heart, is a self-injuring fool. 73. Those whom people called "wicked" that *sannyāsi* used to call "my own people", for, said he, "the extinction of my own evil deeds is taking place through their acts." 74. If any one, therefore, reviled him to his face, his heart used to greatly rejoice. He would exclaim, "Shripati [Krishṇa] is pleased with me. This will easily destroy the sin that is in me ." 75. With such thoughts he kept his peace of mind from being at all shaken, and climbing to the very summit of his courage he sang the following song. Listen to it." 76. Śri Krishṇa said to Uddhava, "For this reason listen with attention. I will relate to you how an intensely avaricious man became one who entirely lost all wordly desires."

THE MISER OF AVANTI.

77. "In the country of Mālava, in the city of Avanti, there lived in his home there a Brahman. He earned his livelihood through agriculture and trade. 78. He possessed an abundance of wealth, grain, and limitless money. But he had a most miserly character. He never even ate sufficiently. 79. What he did eat was poor food, and even of that not a stomach full. Of course, therefore, his wife, children and servants did not have a sufficiency for their stomachs. 80. He never performed the regular religious rites or those prescribed for occasions. Not even in his dreams did he ever do an act of charity. Gods, Brahmans and guests turned away hungry. 81. If he saw an opportunity for gaining a single *kavaḍi,* he would even neglect the *shrāddha* ceremony for his maternal and paternal ancestors, and go even to the house of an outcaste, paying no regard to the fear of being defiled. 82. Through his love of money he lost the recognition of his being of high caste, and the other being an outcaste. So that, if he saw any gain coming to hand, he would even accept the food of an outcaste. 83. Because of his love of money, he did not consider a sin as a great fault. The love of even a *kavaḍi* made him a fool. He did not bring to mind his great impending fall into Hell. 84. Thus he became neglectful of duties, a doer of evil deeds, an ignorer of religious rites, a great knave, a great swindler, a pure rascal, and a lover of money. 85. If there came from any one an hindrance to his obtaining wealth, his anger raged, and he was quite ready to kill even a Brahman or a cow (to accomplish his purpose). 86. Anger has its abode in a lover of wealth. Sins are

associated with wealth. He who is a lover of wealth is known as one of miserly character. 87. This miser accumulated immense wealth, but it was like giving up his very life to spend of it even what was necessary. He had no other thought (but wealth). 88. Just as one cannot extract the kernels of *harabara* grain from out of the mouth of a monkey, so long as it is alive, so to spend any money whatever was like death to this miser. 89. Lest any of the rice for domestic use should be otherwise spent, no part of it went for an offering to the fire. Hence if a guest happened to come, who was there to pay him reverence, at any time! 90. But if a guest was announced, he would utter such words as would kill by the very hearing of them. Who then would think of asking of him water or food? 91. *Brahmachāris* looked at his house with indifference. *Sannyāsis* gave up all expectation, and felt toward him as a royal swan feels towards cowdung. 92. Beggars ceased to pass his door. Chance guests ever left him aside. Visitors sought lodgings at a distance elsewhere, and the Heavenly Ancestors had no hopes at all for food. 93. No one came to his door for uncooked rice. The rats left the house. The crows flew away from his abode. Sparrows could find no grain. 94. Ants had to continually fast, and they too had to change their lodgings to another place. If he would not eat sufficiently himself, what would naturally befall his household? 95. Where the lord of the house is unwilling to eat so much as parched *harbarā*, even though keenly hungry, what must be the plight of the servants in such a house! Even wife and children fainted from hunger. 96. After having vomited, he would not even eat fruit, for he could not bear the thought of such expense. Rather he chose to fast. 97. This avaricious man never honoured his family *guru*, never carried out the family religious duties, never gave a feast to his relatives, never paid respect to his sons-in-law, nor his children's fathers-in-law. 98. At harvest time, even when fruits were abundant, he only saw them with his eyes in the market-place, but under no circumstance would he ever allow them to touch his tongue. 99. He did suck his mother's breast (when a child), but that was the only milk his tongue ever tasted. For after that this avaricious man held to his resolution to absolutely refuse milk. 100. A sweet juice is the mother-home of the tongue. Without it the tongue suffers distress, but his avariciousness was so cruel that he quarreled with his own tongue, not allowing it and any sweet juice to come together. 101. His clothes were dirty and in tatters. His head was always unclean. His breath was offensive, for even in his dreams he would not chew the *pānsupāri*. 102. On festivals, special days, *divāli* and *dasarā* he furnished his household with old *jondhalā* grain. He let his children suffer from lack of food. The name Miser fitted him exactly."

FAMILY AND FRIENDS TURN AGAINST THE MISER.

103. Seeing him thus avaricious, irreligious and miserly in character, his own relations turned against him. How this happened Hari [Krishṇa] relates as follows.

104. "One who lacks all inclination to the performance of his special religious duties. One who cuts off all former givings to others, such an one is an extremely avaricious man, and men speak of him as an ill-natured man. 105. One who not only leaves his family

without food and clothing, but himself also, and will even maltreat himself, is indeed rightly called a miser. 106. It is especially a wife who turns against her miser husband, but so also do relatives, servants and children turn against such. 107. Even his own brothers become opposed to such, and start continual quarrels in the division of wealth. 108. Although with unmeasured wealth in his possession, yet never even inviting his married daughter back to the home on any festal occasion; in her anger she hotly cursed him. 109. His relatives think to themselves, "It would be a good thing if he died, we could then at least enjoy rice and milk." Those of his own kin become his enemies. All begin to wish him evil."

GHOST-PROTECTED WEALTH.

110. The wealth that does not have the protection of right use, soon wastes away. Just how, Hari relates as follows.

111. "Just as a ghost neither eats, nor gives to eat, of buried wealth, nor puts forth his hands to use it any way, just so is it with a miser's buried wealth. He stands guard over his house as does a ghost over buried wealth. 112. An avaricious man, without any love for performing the duties of life, is like a ghost. His wealth is called ghost-wealth, for he regards his property as dearer to him than his own life. 113. The miser allows himself no bodily enjoyments; therefore, his earthly existence becomes of no value. And as his own proper religious duties, and the Five-Sacrificial-Acts are unperformed, his life hereafter becomes also of no value."

THE FIVE SACRIFICIAL ACTS.

114. There are five to whom the sacrifice of wealth is to be made. [God, Spirits, Rishis, Ancestral Beings, and Mankind]. If these do not receive their share of the sacrifice, these five partners become angry, and are ready to destroy that wealth. 115. Although one attains the noblest birth of Brahmanhood, yet through avariciousness fails in his religious and social duties, he becomes a fallen being in both worlds (this and the hereafter), and has to pass through suffering because of his miserliness. 116. With great effort one may collect earthly wealth, but because of unrighteous living, destruction comes upon him. Just how, Hari relates as follows:—

THE FIVE PARTNERS OF WEALTH.

117. "If one neglects the goddesses (presiding over) the Five-Sacrificial-Acts, by his failure he cuts away the root cause through which wealth is acquired. 118. The acquisition of wealth through good deeds may be likened to the glorious sun. When the sun, as right acquisition of wealth sets, Darkness, as wrong use of wealth becomes intense. 119. If to the wealth heaped up by great effort, there comes the night with its darkness of unrighteousness, the goddesses of the Five-Sacrificial-Acts become angry, and then in five ways that wealth is destroyed. 120. He who does not make his own family happy; He who does not give pleasure to himself through various enjoyments, and he who does not spend his money in acts of charity, against him the five-claimants of wealth become aroused. 121. These five are, Relatives, Thieves, the King, Fire, and Disease through wrong living.

These five claimants of wealth come forward to destroy wealth. 122. He who does not show reverence to Brahmans with due devotion; he who does not perform the proper public religious rites; He who does not give in charity as prescribed in the *Vedas,* the destruction of his wealth becomes a certainty. 123. Where no respect is paid to one's parents, where the Five-Great-Sacrificial-Acts are unperformed; where disrespect is paid to one's *guru,* there expect destruction, O Uddhava. 124. They who hate others; they who insult others; they who are swollen with the pride of wealth, the destruction of their wealth will always take place, O Uddhava."

THE MISER LOSES HIS WEALTH.

125. Now the ways in which the destruction of the miser's wealth took place is described to his *bhaktas,* with scriptural authority by Śri Krishṇa Himself, perfect in His compassion, as follows:—

126. "The Miser's wife and sons, conspiring together, made away with some of his secreted money. All of his clan joined together and forcibly divided some of his wealth among themselves. 127. Burglars broke into his house and took away his store of treasures. His house took fire, and an immense amount of his property was destroyed. 128. Pests destroyed his grain fields. He suddenly failed in his business affairs. Those he trusted made away with what was entrusted to them. His promissory notes were lost. 129. As camphor placed in jars evaporates, as ships are lost at sea, so misfortunes fell also on his partners. There was disaster on every side. 130. Swindlers got

hold of him in private and passed false coin on him. Because of this passion of love of money, he allowed the wealth he had to get into their hands. 131. In the conflicts between his own country's armies and those of outside enemies, his house was dug into; his treasures hid in the cellar were removed, carried away by the baskets full. 132. Rain leaked into his grain cellars and rotted all his grain. Violent men contended with him and took away his fields. He became thus one smitten by Fate. 133. Diseases attacked the cattle in his stables. His herds of cows and buffaloes died. He who took away his stable horses, without paying for them, fell on the battle field in the great war.

134. Those who bury treasures in the ground dig up the soil, drawing it up towards them. Then placing the treasure in the hole cover the mouth of it with the earth. 135. Reason, however, often says, "mark the mouth of the hole with a stone." For after having thus absolutely obliterated the place of the hidden treasure, there comes a time when they desire to repossess themselves of the treasure. 136. But the miser now found that the earth itself had entirely swallowed up all his various hidden treasures. Fortune had so turned against him that he could not find the place where he had buried them.

THE MISER'S BODILY APPEARANCE CHANGES.

137. By wrong doing his good fortune was wasting away. Even his bodily appearance now seemed deformed. His complexion even changed. His Brahmanhood became unrecognizable. 138. Those who looked at him would say

"Of what caste are you"? Although he would reply, "I am a Brahman", the hearer would not accept the answer, for the marks of caste superiority had disappeared. 139. Thus all his wealth became totally destroyed, and the nobility of his Brahmanhood was lost. He was now sad of countenance, poor, humiliated, marked by sorrow, and the intensity of grief.

THE MISER BECOMES A DESPISED MAN.

140. His fields were now gone; his ancestral lands had disappeared; his very house was in ruins through the ravages of the enemy army. All his wealth was destroyed, not a *kavaḍi* being left. Such disaster was the natural result of wrong doing. 141. There had been no discharge of his rightful duties, no giving to others, and no use of his wealth for purposes scripturally prescribed. And so the property of this avaricious man vanished, just like the wealth which a poor man possesses in his dreams. 142. Fortune turned against him. Behold the sad condition of that unfortunate man! Wife and children turned against him, and peremptorily drove him away. 143. Notice! This avaricious man, to begin with, had no intimate outside friends, and what pleasure could his own family relations take in him? With disrespect they also drove him away from them. 144. People insulted him to his face. Women and children spat on him. He could get nothing whatever to eat. He begged, but received nothing. 145. Wherever he attempted to beg for food they would say "You ill-starred swretch! What have you come here for? You were deceived by the love of wealth. God has well robbed you of it now! 146. Thus people spurned him. With the loss of wealth he

became a beggar. He fell into a whirlpool of anxiety. Sorrow upon sorrow came upon him.

THE MISER REPENTS.

147. Although the wealth of this avaricious man had vanished, yet the memory of that wealth had not vanished. As he thought of it, his heart was torn to pieces. Through intense grief his mind was in a turmoil. 148. This turmoil, through intense grief, was just like the writhings of a serpent when a thorn has pierced its head, or like that of a lizard when its tail is broken off, or like that of a fish out of water. 149. As he thought of his lost wealth he broke out into sobs. Streams of tears flowed from his eyes. He frequently fainted away. 150. In his mental grief he chafed and fumed. At times he would weep bitterly. He would stand up, sit down, look about, fall down, roll on the ground, sputtering all the while, and making a loud outcry. 151. Then finally he would exclaim "Alas! Alas! Now indeed I have become a child of misfortune. O Brahmadeva, you malicious being! What evil fortune have you written on my forehead? 152. I have now no home anywhere. I cannot think what is to become of me in the future." And with this thought of the intense sorrow that had fallen upon him, this very sad man burst into crying. 153. "And yet" he said to himself "This pain that I suffer here in this life is but small. A greater pain awaits me hereafter. Yama will cruelly beat me. Who will deliver me from Him?. 154. I have given nothing of my wealth to others. I have not remembered Nārāyana [God]. Now the terrors of Hell are before me. Who there will deliver me? 155. I have not performed the Five-great-sacrificial-acts. I gave no food to unexpected guests. I per-

formed no sacrifice for the fathers-in-Heaven. Now who will save me from my distress? 156. I did not show reverence to Brahmans. I did not worship Adhokshaja [Vishṇu]. I did not bow down to the dust of the feet of the Vaishṇava saints. Who will now destroy my accumulated sorrow? 157. I am altogether a wrong doer. I am sinking! I am sinking into a horrible pit! O hasten, and come to me, O Śri Hari! Save me, a poor wretch! 158. Krishṇa, Mādhava, Murāri, Ananta, Śri Hari, Thou-of-the-Eagle-Baner, Thou-who-held-up-Mount Govardhana, save me! a poor wretch. 159. Thou didst protect Pralhād. Thou didst protect Amba Rishi from lying in the womb. Thou didst care for Parikshiti while in the womb. So save me a poor wretch. 160. Thou didst save Ahalyā. Thou didst save the sinful Ajāmila. Thou didst leap to the help of Gajendra. So with that same haste rush to save me. 161. By Thy name Thou didst save that vile pimp [Piṅgalā], whose life was a course of greatest sins. So O Chakrapāṇi [Krishṇa], by that same miraculous power save me, a wretched sinner! 162. Damn! Damn! this desire for wealth! Because of it my life has been spent in vain. The name of Rām, free without cost, I, a vile wretch, did not repeat. 163. By the power of Rām's name ten millions of great sins are burnt away. But I, the one great vile wretch of the universe, did not repeat his name with my lips."

THE MISER'S SELFCONDEMNATION.

164. Thus recognizing his transgression, he repented with deep sorrow. And there arose in him an intense loathing of worldly objects. How he expressed it, Govinda [Krishṇa] relates as follows.

165. Wringing his hands, he cried "Alas! Alas! Possession of a Brahman's body is a part of the scheme of salvation. Yet though attaining it, I, a vile miser, have been deceived through the trickery of the love of wealth. 166. I have given pain to that Brahman body, through which it is possible to enjoy the happiness of salvation. A lover of wealth, I am a supreme fool. There is no other fool greater than I am. 167. Instead of spending my wealth in benevolence, I wasted my efforts in adding wealth to wealth. And now this is the result of my possessions. It has brought me the fruit of bitter sorrow. 168. What a great marvel is this love of money! It gives you neither this life nor the next. The happiness of present salvation is lost, and there is before one the suffering of an unescapable Hell. 169. Behold a Hell so deep, that if one should sink in it for a whole *kalpa,* one would not reach its bottom. Into such a Hell the love of money casts one, and I have added that Hell to my human life. 170. He who is born with a Brahman body is honoured in the Three-worlds. Salvation bows at his feet. But I, unfortunate wretch, have wasted my opportunity. 171. The wealth which I heaped up through the love of it, has altogether disappeared. It has made me supremely miserable. It has bound me, and given me over to Great Hell. 172. I received a superior birth. I have made it of no account through this love of money. Now in the midst of the fierce fire of remorse I see my life as already passed away. 173. By my excessive love of money all my strenuous efforts have ended in vain. But I now feel an intense disgust of wordly things arising in me, very sincere and reasonable. 174. I now feel that an avaricious man is a

vessel fit for every sort of pain. A slave to wealth is a low wretch indeed!" Thus with his own lips he reviled himself.

THE CONVERTED MISER DENOUNCES AVARICE.

175. " It is a general rule that a slave to wealth has no happiness in this life. In the act of protecting his wealth he suffers intensely, and if it leaves him, it is like death to him. 176. In accumulating wealth there are great difficulties. In protecting it also there are great conflicts with others. In the loss of wealth there comes a breaking of the heart. A lover of money has to suffer in this life. 177. And not only has he suffering in this life, but because of his wrong doings, his way is blocked for the Life-to-come. When the lover of wealth dies, Hell of a certainty crushes down upon his breast. 178. He who will not give in charity to others, nor even eat properly himself; he who is a miser, as I have been, has only increasing pain before him. A miser can hope for no happiness or comfort. 179. Where the lust for money has its abode there is no happiness even in one's dreams. Lust for money is most contemptible." This the miser also explained with his own lips.

THE CONVERTED MISER ILLUSTRATES THE EVIL OF AVARICE

180. "A chieftain falls on the battle field. Some one rushes forward, fighting his way into the midst of the conflict, and brings away the king on his shoulder. This act brings him great renown. 181. But avarice steals into his heart. He asks the king for the gift of a field, as his

reward. This request brings him discredit, and the world laughs at his foolishness. 182. Unasked by him, the king was perhaps about to give him a position equal to his own, but this avarice of his brought him loss of every thing, and made known the foolishness of his character.

183. A man, in giving his daughter in marriage makes his whole family holy. But if through avarice that avaricious man accepts money in the giving away of his daughter, a fall into Hell is his lot.

184. A giver gives a gift, but if through it he gains in return, that is a blot on the giver, and his avariciousness is a blemish on the gift.

185. One studies the *Vedas* and other *Shāstras*, and becomes a most learned pandit. Then the lust for wealth brings him trouble. He becomes proud of his knowledge. 186. Then to gain self-glorification the pandit becomes a controversialist with other pandits, and uses irritating language in his opposition to them. Thus the very wise even are deceived by avarice. 187. Avarice can bring even a right-thinking wise philosopher into utter contempt. If this be true of him, how much more true of others. They end by becoming the slaves of avarice. 188. Avarice turns a pure man into an impure. Where there is avarice there are aroused feelings of contempt. Listen to some clear illustrations of this which I shall relate.

189. Of noble family, most lovely in form, altogether attractive, but on the nose appears a small white spot of leprosy. Now her beauty is lost sight of in contempt. 190. So if the slightest spot of avarice finds a place, it spoils nobility of character, generosity, victory and good repute.

There is nothing in the Three-Worlds that brings such disrepute as does Avarice. 191. With lust of wealth there is always contention. Lust for wealth breaks the bonds of closest brotherhood. There is no such supremely vile pest as Lust for wealth.

WEALTH BRINGS ANXIETIES.

192. In the first place one has to labor hard to accumulate wealth. In the second place one has to labor hard to increase it. And even if one's wealth has grown enormously, yet Avarice never says "It is enough." 193. If men but labored for the *Supreme-Spiritual-Riches [*Paramārtha*] as they everywhere do so heartily for earthly riches, the acquisition of Brahma [God] would be but play. 194. But because the acquisition of wealth is thus connected with painful effort, and because to protect it requires intense anxiety of mind, it becomes a great strain on life, a care day and night. 195. These money lovers are unable to trust wife or child, nor even mother or father. For the care of their property they are unable to place confidence in any one but themselves. 196. Indifferent to possible injury to his own person he has to protect his property from the thief who would steal it from him. In thus guarding his property his mind has to be for ever concentrated on the three conditions of wealth [acquisition, increase and protection]. 197. If such concentration of mind were but devoted to the worship of God, in half a moment, Chakrapāṇi

---

*Supreme-Spiritual Riches, a literal translation of *Paramārtha,* which signifies the highest spiritual state that can be attained.

[Krishṇa] would yield to the wish of the Seeker. 198. Whether money is spent for legitimate or illegitimate purposes, connected with marriages, or even spent for one's own stomach, there is always intense anxiety. Even the use of money creates concern. 199. And so while acquiring and protecting wealth, if sudden destruction comes to it, the mind of the bond-slave of wealth, in his craze for wealth, is thrown into violent turmoil. 200. In the acquiring of money there is painful effort. In the protecting of money there dwells anxiety. In the spending of money there is a round of trouble, and in the loss of wealth comes utter confusion. 201. Thus at its beginning, at its middle and at its end wealth is altogether a cause of evil. There is not the slightest happiness in it. Such has been the relation of wealth to myself."

FIFTEEN GREAT EVILS FROM LOVE OF RICHES.

202. The confusion that accompanies wealth, together with its drudgery, its troubles and anxieties, and the fact that the greater the riches the greater the disaster when they are lost, is described by the miser himself, as follows:

203. "Viewed from all sides, it is seen that riches bring evil. This saying of mine is absolutely true. All the evils in the world grow out of riches. 204. If one asks what are the evils arising from riches, they are too uncountable and infinite to be numerated. Yet I will describe here in brief fifteen of the evils that come from riches.

THEFT, THE FIRST EVIL FROM LOVE OF RICHES.

205. The first evil from riches is theft in relation to wealth. He who has no riches has no fear of a thief. 206. It is rather the thief who is afraid when he sees one without any money, and conceals himself for fear that the poor man will ask him for something.

207. To rob, by claiming a mysterious second sight, to strip another of his all by claims of alchemy, to fleece another of his money through his simplicity, to rob one of all in some uninhabited place, (are acts arising from the love of money) 208. Something of value belonging to another is fallen in the road. Knowing that it belongs to a certain person, and yet not to return it to him;—these are examples of Theft.

209. Although Hell is the final end of one who steals gold, yet there are even intelligent men guilty of this kind of theft. If they steal, how much more likely are others to do the same. The home of Theft is with Wealth. 210. In this world Theft is the greatest sinner. No one allows her to sit even at his door. She has to live where there is gold. Where there is wealth, there you will find Theft. 211. Even a *sannyāsi,* looking on wealth may have his heart turned. Then what must be its effect on others? Theft always lives close to wealth. 212. The first great evil effect of wealth is therefore that Theft is connected with it.

MURDER, THE SECOND EVIL FROM LOVE OF RICHES.

Wealth is the abode of even murder. Listen to a description of this. 213. Connected with wealth are fierce quarrels. Some even murder their sons and grandsons. For gaining wealth some, throwing aside friendship, take the lives of friends. 214. One of the strange things arising from the lust for wealth is that a daughter should give poison to her father, and feel no grief over killing him. So cruel is lust for wealth! 215. This lust for wealth makes some discard their fathers and mothers, and live apart from them with their wives. But there also notice this same result from the lust for wealth, in the enmity between that man and his wife. 216. O the strangeness of this lust for wealth, that a son should kill his father! That a father should murder his son! O the lust for wealth is indeed cruel! 217. A son, for the sake of money, will murder his mother, who for nine months had carried him in her womb! and had to suffer the unpleasant duties connected with his care. 218. The power of the lust for wealth is indeed strange! How can I even describe its extraordinary character, such as that a mother should kill the son of her own womb. Such are the evil deeds men will commit for money. 219. Thus Murder is the climax of the second evil."

UNTRUTH, THE THIRD EVIL FROM LOVE OF RICHES.

The miser himself now describes Untruth as an effect of the love of riches. 220. "Untruth is born from the womb of Riches. Through the power of riches Untruth has become very mighty in this universe. With riches Untruth rises to power. Where riches are, there you find Untruth. 221. Wherever any one has riches, or wherever any one has a desire for riches, there Untruth with all its kin will be found, and he becomes a rightful heir to this wealth in the form of Untruth. 222. Untruth gains its strength from riches. It makes a son lie to his father. Through the lust for wealth he deceives even his mother. Truth does not exist where wealth is. 223. The common people tell untruths in their buying and selling. But even those learned in the *Vedas* and other *shāstras,* and wise men will tell untruths for gaining wealth. 224. Although unable to recite correctly the words of the *Vedas,* yet for the sake of getting money, one will say, in performing a sacrifice for those of low caste, "I am learned in the *Vedas.*" 225. Giving a bribe to an intermediary, they claim to be celebrated scholars of the four *Vedas.* With the idea of getting money from the king, pandits even are plagued by Untruth. 226. One claims to have no worldly desires, and to be a seeker after the Supreme-Spiritual-Riches. But here Untruth makes its abode. He pretends to accomplishments that are false, for the sake of worldly riches. 227. Untruth reaches its climax in connection with wealth. Some one in perfect devotion goes to a *guru,* but in private teaches him false and atheistic doctrines (for the sake of gain). 228. One who possesses no worldly riches, and has no thought for worldly riches, such an one Untruth never touches, even to the end of the world." 229. Thus the connection of Untruth with riches has now been described.

HYPOCRISY, THE FOURTH EVIL FROM LOVE OF RICHES.

Listen now, that you may recognize the connection of Hypocrisy with wealth. 230." Without having in his heart the Supreme-Spiritual-Riches, and selfishly grasping after worldly riches, and yet calling himself a *bhakta* of Hari, such an one is rightly called a hypocrite in his worship. 231. He who for the sake of adding to his wealth wears the mark on the forehead, carries a rosary, and wears the breast-marks, or preaches for the sake of gain, he is known to be a hypocrite, with only an outer stamp of sincerity. 232. He who looks at a wealthy man of high position, and in his preaching to him manifests extreme humility, but gives to him the initiatory *mantras,* only after fixing a definite sum for his fee as a *guru,* is a hypocrite. 233. A *guru,* who shows affection for an influential disciple, because he possesses wealth, and neglects a poor disciple, is an illustration of an hypocritical *guru.* 234. A *guru* who preaches that one should give to his *guru* body, soul, and property, and then accumulates wealth, is also an illustration of an hypocritical *guru.* 235. If a *guru* has the lust for wealth, how can he by his teachings save his disciples? Such is the characteristic of lust for riches, that it can make even a *guru* a hypocrite.

236. Among all existing creatures the most rascally hypocrite is the disciple who pretends to be humble, and receives instruction from his *guru,* with the purpose of making away with his *guru's* property. 237. A disciple who gains knowledge from his *guru,* and then becomes so proud of his own knowledge, that he regards his *guru* as

merely a common man, he also is certainly a hypocrite. 238. The disciple who says "I am the one wealthy and wise," and with this pride of puny knowledge despises the teachings of his *guru,* he also is an illustration of an hypocrite. 239. Where there is the claim "I am Brahma" but where there is not really the experience of oneness with Brahma, there this vulgar claim "I am a knower of Brahma" comes from a subtle hypocrisy.

240. The body holds a middle place in one's life, and is the chief abiding place of hypocrisy. Now add to this the *mana* *[mind], and we get pride of knowledge. 241. The acts of hypocrisy are very strange. For example, "I am an *agnihotri.* I am a priest" says one, and gains his livelihood thereby, Thus by their lust for wealth the repeaters of the *Vedas* are overcome by the lust of riches. 242. Even those who open the book that teaches of the Supreme-Spiritual-Riches, and in various ways preach the Knowledge of Brahma, even those wise men are harrassed by hypocrisy. The lust for wealth creates an intense desire for money. 243. Of what value are other *mantras* and *tantras,* when Brahmans abuse the *Gāyatri mantra,* and hypocritically say, "We are true to our religious duties, We are pure". 244. Hypocrisy works the ruin even of a *sannyāsi,* for he has to observe social etiquettes. They make him forget the

---

*Mind is the soul functioning in thinking, imagining, willing and memory. *Mana* is regarded as an organ [*Indriya*] of thinking, imagining, willing and memory, and is not the *ātmā* [soul] itself. The distinction is important, hence I have retained the Marathi word *mana,* instead of its mistranslation, mind.

purpose for which he has had his head shaved. 245. If the *sannyāsi* performs his cleansings and baths, thinking the while of food and honor, he is not able to cleanse his own heart, and his lectures on the *Vedas* are very hypocritical.

246. This fourth evil of Hypocrisy is thus defined as that of falsely pretending to goodness in order to receive money and food from others, or for the purpose of gaining outward honour.

SENSUALITY, THE FIFTH EVIL OF LOVE OF RICHES.

247. With money is associated sensuality. Where wealth is excessive, and beyond the common reach, there will be found a riot of wild sensuality. 248. Even if one is without money, one is afflicted with sensuality, which within and without brings him trouble, and has to endure the ups and downs of many forms of severe and difficult experiences. 249. But when wealth comes, then unbridled sensuality leads him to illegitimate intercourse. It begets in the rich man many forms of wrong doing, and contemptible deeds. 250. When sensuality is thus associated with wealth, it always brings trouble to the rich. Sensuality, with wealth, stirs up passions day and night. 251. Thus sensuality, associated with wealth, becomes at times exceedingly wild." Such is the Fifth evil.

ANGER, THE SIXTH EVIL FROM LOVE OF RICHES.

"Wherever there are sensual desires there most certainly will be found Anger with all his hosts. 252. If anything comes in the way of fulfilling one's desires, Anger leaps to the front. Stirred up into excessive violence Anger destroys the efficacy of scores of acts of austerities. 253. One may have wasted oneself away in acquiring a condition that is most difficult, through the repetition of God's names, austerities, worship, and the performance of prescribed duties. But Anger, when supremely stirred, will in half a moment turn all to ashes. 254. If anyone points even a finger at one's wealth, furious Anger arises. It may even arise to murderous proportions. Anger, associated with wealth, may become exceedingly wicked. 255. Any obstruction to the acquisition of wealth, as well as any opposition in its use, is an opportunity for the stirring up of Anger, intensely antagonistic and domineering. 256. Anger, when associated with wealth, is thus very powerful." This is the Sixth most evil result.

PRIDE, THE SEVENTH EVIL FROM THE LOVE OF RICHES.

With wealth is to be found extraordinary Pride. This, the Miser describes, as follows. 257. "When Pride of wealth has swollen, a son will not look even at his father. He will even say to his mother "You low wretch". Then what must he say to others! 258. Seeing saints, *sādhus,* and ascetics, he laughs at them, saying "It is the low wretches who become *sannyāsis*". He despises even the *Haridās.* 259. If to the might of wealth be added that of knowledge then the arrogance of Pride comes to its full, just as a boa constrictor would stiffen up if he were to swallow a post. 260. Look how the Pride of wealth, joined to the Pride of knowledge, affects even one's relation to a *sadguru.* There is first the neglect of his teachings, and finally contempt and scorn for the *guru* himself. 261. The characteristic of Pride of wealth, joined to Pride of knowledge, is that of looking for faults in one's *sadguru,* calling his *sadguru* a fool, and regarding himself as the one only wise person. 262. He calls his *sadguru* an idiot. He hates even him who pays regard to his *guru.* Bāp!! What a strange thing Pride is in thus looking for the faults of all others. 263. The ways of Pride are indeed curious. It never acknowledges the good in others as true. The moment it hears of a fault in others it regards it as most certainly true. 264. A good man comes into the presence of a proud man. Pride makes the latter regard the former as untrue. If he sees before him an exceedingly good man, he regards him as crazy and a simpleton. 265. Only when the proud man is seized with intense dizziness, and falling, strikes the ground with his forehead, does he make a *sāshtāṅg namaskār,* for to his proud vision he finds no one in particular in the Universe worthy of a bow. 266. Thus dizzy with Pride, what honor does he ever give to greatness! What respect to age! Stiffened through pride of wealth he regards himself as the one only great personage in the universe. 267. Take the case even of one who is faithfully serving his *guru.* He may be seduced by his own service. He may become proud of his own service, a spirit very injurious to a servant." 268. Such is the intoxication of Pride. Pride is thus an evil of the seventh form.

ARROGANCE, THE EIGHTH EVIL FROM THE LOVE OF RICHES.

With wealth there is also Arrogance. The Brahman miser relates the effects of it as follows.

269. "He, in whom the arrogance of wealth arises, is blind, though with open eyes. He has ears, but listens not to the voice of instruction. Through the arrogance of wealth he becomes indifferent. 270. Through this arrogance of wealth comes extreme self-conceit. Through this arrogance of wealth comes impudence. Through this arrogance of wealth comes every kind of unlawful deeds. 271. Arrogance of wealth is most unholy. If it swells up in one, it becomes exceedingly hard to control. It leads him to strange relationships, without regard to the worthy or the unworthy. 272. He who is the victim of Arrogance of wealth fears no one. He goes where he should not go. He eats to his heart's content what he should not eat. 273. He associates with those with whom he should not associate. He does what he should not do. He utters what he should not utter. In the assemblies of men he manifests his impudence. 274. He pays no attention to his own deeds, and accuses others. He does not listen to his father's intruction. His arrogance makes him insane. 275. He will not listen to what he has been taught. He insists on doing what he has been told not to do. In his ranting he even insults *sadhus* to his heart's content. 276. He pays no regard to his own caste duties, or to his own personal duties. He pays no regard to violation of caste rules, or to misconduct. He pays no consideration to the ideas of his elders. He becomes intoxicated by the arrogance of wealth. 277. To begin with, he may be in the flush of youth. On top of that comes the insolence of the arrogance of wealth. In this way he becomes highly intoxicated, and so no longer walks in the good path. 278. He becomes overcome with sexual desires, and pays no regard to family or character, or to proper occasions. He acts just like an ass. 279.

Lusting after women he makes his way to them even in daylight. He goes even after widows. He has no fear of sin. 280. When a man is intoxicated by drinking liquor, that intoxication very soon disappears, but the intoxication from wealth is more enduring, for even with death it does not disappear. 281. That doing wrong brings self-inflicted death, this the wrong doer does not remember. He is deceived by his arrogance of wealth. 282. Arrogance of wealth is thus connected with great evils." These are characteristics of the eighth evil.

DISUNION, THE NINTH EVIL FROM THE LOVE OF RICHES.

With wealth comes Disunion to the full. The Brahman miser describes it as follows.

283. "Disunion is born from the womb of wealth. Where wealth is there is its rightful place. Disunion lives with wealth, with all its retinue, awake day and night. 284. Great wealth perhaps comes to some one. He will keep it a secret from his own mother. He will deceive his father about it, and will not even tell his wife of it. 285. A son is unaware of the wealth of his father, then how much less will others know of it. There is nothing that creates Disunion in this world everywhere as does wealth. 286. A man who will help his brother on the battle field, and bear the stroke of the sword on his own head, even he, when the spoils are being divided, will act as though he was no relative of his. 287. A friend will give his life for his friends, but when money enters into their affairs it brings suspicions into their friendship. Bitter Disunion accompanies wealth. 288. The wealth one holds in one's possession has to be

frequently watched. To such lengths goes suspicion when wealth is concerned. 289. Such is the Disunion that accompanies wealth." This is the characteristic of the ninth evil.

ENMITY, THE TENTH EVIL FROM THE LOVE OF RICHES.

With wealth comes strong and exceedingly bitter enmity. 290. Enmity comes to its full in connection with wealth. The Brahman miser having personally experienced it, gives illustrations of the Enmity that accompanies wealth.

291. "Money considerations bring about contentions between father and son. They make enemies of one's own brothers. This is a well known effect of the lust for wealth. 292. Lust for wealth stirs up quarrels between very dear friends. Such quarrels over wealth are the bitterest, and involve every one. 293. Lust for wealth will turn a friend, whom you love more than your own life, into an enemy. Lust for wealth is most unholy, an enemy hard to overcome in this world. 294. In the divisions of wealth quarrels arise among brothers, because one thinks he should receive more, and those good people who are dividing the property justly, they even become the objects of enmity. 295. Some, because of their lust for wealth, will cherish deep enmity against the mother who bore them, and whose breasts they sucked. 296. Riches may make one an enemy of one's own mother, and he may turn her out of his house, refusing to see her face again. 297. Pride of wealth brings alienation from the *sadguru*, through whose teachings the bondage of this world is broken, and purity is attained. 298. The might

of the lust for wealth is seen in enmity towards *sadgurus* themselves. Where there is pride of wealth there is no friendship to be found with any one. 299. That which has been described is Enmity in its fulness." This is the characteristic of the tenth evil.

DISTRUST, THE ELEVENTH EVIL FROM THE LOVE OF RICHES.

"With wealth comes Distrust. Listen! 300. As one effect of the pride of wealth is that a son does not trust his father. He wholly distrusts his brothers. How much less will he trust his friends. 301. "My son is myself" is a saying, and he is in fact lord of all in the home, yet the father will not trust his son. Lust for wealth makes one intensely distrustful. 302. She, to whom, at the time of marriage, a solemn promise was given, "Swearing by my ancestors, truly, thrice truly, I will give you my dutiful care, my wealth and my love;" 303. and who in everything has offered up her very life to her husband, lust for wealth makes him distrustful of even such a legally married wife. 304. A son will not trust his own mother, even her who carried him nine months in her womb, and suffered all the unpleasantnesses of his care. 305. One who has this pride of wealth will not trust even his *sadguru*. How much more will he not distrust others. One who is proud of his wealth is absolutely distrustful. 306. The causes of Distrust are, foremost, wealth, and secondly, women. Those whose minds are seduced by these, become eminently distrustful. 307. He who regards wealth, and who is the captive of women, from him, He-who-dwells-in-the-Heart

[God], turns away. His *sadguru* also disregards him. The evils from Distrust are very great.

308. In the *Purāṇas* the chief of all faults is called Distrust. [*avishvās*] If it appears but half a moment, it turns all good intentions into dust. 309. When Pride joins Distrust, the Deliverance of the one delivered from the power of this worldly life, is ended, and then by the might of Doubt he is thrown again down into the bodily bondage of life. 310. When Distrust of others has enveloped the mind, Pride says, "I am the one who knows.". Then belief in the existence of God suddenly abandons him, and he sees proofs of His inexistence every where. 311. When Distrust of others comes, then kindly feeling, and all it includes, flee away. And then everywhere this total lack of kindly feeling accompanies all relations with others, through its suspicions. 312. In a strange way suspicions abide with a distrustful man continually. Wherever Distrust enters there suspicion robs him of everything. 313. Distrust easily makes a desert of the Kingdom of the Supreme-Spiritual-Riches. Distrustful, he begins to point out the faults of his *sadguru*. He loses faith in Brahma Itself. 314. Thus there is no king of faults greater than Distrust. Where he enters with determination, he easily conquers even the one who has attained the greatest accomplishments. 315. Wherever Distrust advances, there the search for the Supreme Spiritual Riches has to flee away, When suspicion makes its attack, that is the time one is robbed of all one has. 316. The *sādhu* loses the ornament of his *sādhuhood*. The Seeker to be a *sādhu* is robbed of his all. Ordinary men fill the jungle, for the garden of faith is destroy-

ed. 317. The cities of self-restraint are burned down. Anger makes a bonfire of austerities. The elephant of seduction destroys to their very root the banana trees that were bearing abundantly the fruits of salvation. 318. The cottages of Peace and Self-restraint become torn down and strewn in the bypaths. The squares of Right-Thinking [*viveka*] are deserted. No one longer walks through them. 319. The beauty of rites and fastings; the gardens of Absence-of-desire, are everywhere and in many ways burned up by suspicions. 320. When to such as are proud of their knowledge there comes to visit them the Distrustful, then Suspicion, giving assuring promises, makes them live with itself.

321. Before such Distrust what is poor Supreme-Spiritual-Riches! Suspicion is mighty in power for immediate evil. 322. He who is inherently distrustful is always looking for faults in the character of others. It becomes finally his fixed character to hate the Supreme-Spiritual-Riches. 323. Thus Distrust becomes the determined enemy of the Supreme-Spiritual-Riches. Even should there appear with a smiling face one who is inherently distrustful, the humble should not even approach him. 324. Powerful among all faults, the one that has gained the kingly power among faults, is this eleventh evil from the lust of wealth. 325. It makes all the eleven senses altogether distrustful, therefore, it is given the eleventh place The abode of Distrust is the *mana* [mind]."

RIVALRY, THE TWELFTH EVIL FROM THE LOVE OF RICHES.

326. "The chief abode of Rivalry is with much knowledge or much wealth. This is its birthplace. From here

it begins to grow. 327. When knowledge has become great then Pandits begin to insult Pandits. It especially shows itself in envy against one's *sadguru.* This envious spirit is also connected with knowledge. 328. When one is possessed of wealth, then Rivalry creates great commotion. And he exclaims, "Kuber became rich through the wealth of others, but I am rich through my own power". 329. "The pebbles in the Ganges are few compared with the abundance of my wealth. What poor wretches can stand before the supremacy of my wealth!" 330. So whatever the rich man sees he despises and spurns. Thus Rivalry, possessing itself of great wealth, rejoices. 331. Rivalry is then the twelfth evil connected with the lust for wealth. It ever lives with wealth, as has already been said."

IMMORALITY, GAMBLING AND DRINKING, THE THIRTEENTH, FOURTEENTH, AND FIFTEENTH EVILS FROM THE LOVE OF RICHES.

332. Now there are three evils connected with one another, which may be grouped under one head, but listen to their description in detail. 333. The three are; Prostitution, Gambling and Drinking of intoxicants. Wealth stimulates these three. These three powerful evils especially affect the rich.

334. "A man without wealth is regarded by his wife as a heavy burden. Such a woman, seeing the face of her poor husband, will spit in his face. 335. In the poor man's home there may be a quarrel between the man and the woman. She may insult him in vile language, and drive

him out of the house 336. But in a rich man's house how the woman bows and scrapes, just as a dog barks and wags its tail at the sight of a morsel of food. 337. But let his money be gone, then she goes for him tooth and nail. "Now I do not care for you" she storms in her rage. 338. "I cannot endure by day the nuisance of the children. At night I cannot endure your nagging. You do not now own even a broken *kavaḍi.* Damn the joy of this sort of living!" she exclaims. 339. Thus insulting him in many ways she may drive him out of the house. A man's own wife no longer shows love for a penniless husband. 340. A wife does not remain subject to a penniless husband. The rich man is pestered by women continually day and night.

341. To gain the notice of the rich man the prostitute displays herself with her ornaments, and special gestures, and the rich man is seduced. 342. And when his mind is thus continually seduced through association with prostitutes, he is led by them to Drinking intoxicating liquors, being already intoxicated by wealth.

343. Intoxicated through Drinking intoxicants, such an one Gambles willingly. Thus these three evils are connected with wealth." 344. Thus there are fifteen evils connected with wealth. These have now been described in detail. The wealthy have not the slightest happiness in connection with their wealth.

A BHAKTA SHOULD AVOID RICHES.

345. "These fifteen evils of necessity arise wherever either a fool or a pandit accumulates riches. 346. In name only they are riches; in reality they are evils, therefore the

bhaktas of Hari, who seek after the good, should reject them. 347. Just as the fly cannot endure the odour of myrrh; as the bedbug will not come near oil, or as the ants will not touch the fire, so the *bhakta* does not even touch riches. 348. Just as when salt is thrown into the fire it sputters and flies out, so he who is anxious for Deliverance [*moksha*] will reject his wealth entirely. 349. The poisonous *bachnāg* when taken into one's mouth, tastes sweet for half a moment, but in the end it brings death. Similar is the evil of riches. 350. Therefore he who is anxious for final Deliverance [*moksha*] should not grasp for riches. He should reject riches in all the acts of his body, his speech and his mind.

LOVE OF RICHES A CAUSE OF DIVISIONS.

351. Riches are the root cause of divisions, as has already been described above. Govinda [Krishṇa] again and again clearly asserts this. 352. Wealth, worth but a broken *kavadi*, may break the friendship of the closest friends, may spoil the affection of brother for brother, may destroy good feelings between comrades. 353. Connected with riches is often the strife between father and son, and quarrels between wife and children. They destroy the affection of friends. 354. Twenty *kavaḍi* shells make a *kākiṇi*. One *kākiṇi* may destroy the friendship of relatives. Even one broken *kavaḍi* shell may create a division among friends. 355. For even a very small amount of money one may drop his friendship, and stirred within to anger, may be ready to use an armed fist. 356. In such a case a relative becomes as one not a relative. One destroys the other. Besides being destroyers of one's own good, riches may lead to such evils as murder. 357. In this life riches

work one's evil. When one dies they take one to the gates of Hell.

LUST FOR RICHES MAKES THE NOBLEST BIRTH A FAILURE.

Listen, how riches work the destruction of a noble birth. 358. It requires the good deeds of ten million births to arrive at a human body in this world of action. Birth into the highest caste, into a noble Brahman family, stands supreme. 359. In order to have such a birth even the gods ask for death. Indra, and other gods, who live in Heaven, they also wish for such a birth. 360. Those who have attained to *Satyaloka* [Heaven of Righteousness], and live in wonderful glory, they also earnestly and continually wish for this birth. 361. Here below the worshipper of God has the four forms of Deliverance [*moksha*] worshipping at his feet. It is because of this that the gods ask for this birth continually. 362. Now having attained such a noble Brahman birth, I am the most unfortunate in the Three-Worlds, for I rejected my own good, having been seduced by the lust for wealth, to the acquiring of wealth. 363. He who commits the error of lusting after riches, or who, for the sake of gaining popularity, neglects the worship of God, he has an unhappy end before him. 364. This unhappy ending for the luster after riches is the falling into Hell, the eight million four hundred thousand rebirths, with the intense sufferings of the life in the womb."

ADVANTAGE OF A BRAHMAN BIRTH.

365. How easy is it in a Brahman birth to acquire Heaven and final Deliverance [*moksha*], the Miser relates in detail as follows.

366. "When a Brahman performs the duties special to him, he acquires the desire for Heaven, so that a noble Twice-born easily attains the abode of Indra, the Moon and other gods. 367. The attainment of Heaven by others is through the performance of sacrifices. Heaven being thus in the hands of the Brahman, it is easy for him to attain it. 368. The Brahman who drops the three objects of desire, and performs his special duties, without the desire of reward, Deliverance [*moksha*] stands day and night at his feet, ready to obey his behests. 369. To whomsoever the Brahman shows his favor, such an one attains Deliverance [*moksha*]. Such is the power a Brahman possesses, without effort on his part, and naturally.

LOVE OF RICHES DESTROYS THE BRAHMAN'S ADVANTAGE.

370. Though such is the superiority of the Brahman, to whom Heaven is but a step, and Deliverance [*moksha*], an obedient servant, yet he can be destroyed by the lust for wealth. 371. Having attained a Brahman birth, the succession of births and deaths thereafter could be absolutely stopped. But I have robbed myself of this advantage by acquiring wealth through the lust for wealth 372. To be born a human being is difficult, and most difficult is it to be born a Brahman, but having attained that birth, I have lost all through lust for wealth. 373. Although acquiring a Brahman's body, even great men have been deceived by riches. Wealth is the chief abode of evil. It produces sorrows hard to bear. 374. Because riches are the home of evils, one must entirely cast them aside." And now in

the full heat of his rejection of worldly desires, the Brahman miser, speaks as follows:—

THE FIVE GREAT SACRIFICES OF WEALTH.

375. "But now a question arises. If by fortune one should gain wealth, is he to throw it away into an alley? Or pour it into a stream? How should one get rid of wealth already acquired?" 376. The Brahman miser relates as below how to get rid of riches. Those therefore who are wealthy, let them listen with attention.

377. "If one by fortune has acquired wealth, he should perform the Five Great Sacrifices. [To the Gods, Ancestral Spirits, Living Parents. Brahmans, and Mankind].

THE SACRIFICE OF WEALTH TO GOD.

He should worship God with joy and greatest delight.

THE SACRIFICE OF WEALTH TO ANCESTRAL SPIRITS.

378. One should make offerings to the fathers-in-Heaven. One should save the fathers-in-Heaven by a pilgrimage to Gayā, and performing there the ninety-six *shrāddha* ceremonies.

THE SACRIFICE OF WEALTH TO LIVING PARENTS.

379. While one's parents are living, one owes them obeisance thrice a day, and never should one treat them with disrespect. Never should one show them disrespect even at the danger of one's own life. 380. One should

honor them, give them such food as pleases them; give them money according to one's ability, and through service make them supremely happy. 381. One's father is God, Nārāyaṇa Himself. One's mother is goddess Lakshmi Herself. He who with this feeling honors them is to be recognized as a good son. 382. The true Sacrifice to parents is the service that makes them happy. One who shows disrespect to them, while they are living, his idea of the *shrāddha* ceremony, when they are dead, is simply a public form. 383. He who is untrue to his father's wish is guilty of a great pile of sins. He who is true to his father's wishes, Final-Deliverance [*moksha*] is a servant at his feet." 384. The worship due to parents, whether living or dead, has now been described in full, and to which one may give the name of Parent-worship.

THE SACRIFICE OF WEALTH TO BRAHMANS.

And now listen to Rishi-worship! 385. "The bringing of a Brahman into one's home with tokens of respect, honoring him, washing his feet, paying homage to the water in which his feet have been washed, all this should be done mentally and physically. 386. He should be worshipped with incense and lights, satisfying his appetite with dainty food, and giving him money according to one's ability. This is called Rishi-worship. 387. A Brahman is Lord-of-Rishis. The Sanatkumāra [sons of Brahmadeva], are satisfied if Brahmans are satisfied. Śārangdhara [Krishṇa] belched through the Brahman's mouth in satisfaction for the food he received."

THE SACRIFICE OF WEALTH TO MANKIND.

388. "The kind of giving that stands the highest is that to brothers, to those of one's own immediate family, and relatives, giving them of one's wealth to relieve them of the hard misery of their poverty. 389. To let one's own family suffer, while giving food or money to others, is absolutely wrong. It is not an act of pure goodness. 390. But having made all of one's own immediate family properly happy, the balance that remains should be spent for the good of others. 391. If, for example, a chance guest arrives, one should give him food without fail. If he has to turn his face away from you, that entirely takes away from you your good deeds. 392. Among all forms of giving, the giving of food is the noblest. To the poor one should show respect, and give him food courteously. 393. While making one's own immediate family happy, while giving food to the poor generously, to treat one's own life in a miserly way, that also is a grievous wrong. 394. One should give to satisfy the needs of the poor, but as each one is himself one of the poor, there should be no partiality shown in serving. All should share alike in the serving of food. 395. To show partiality in the treatment to dining guests is a grievous fault. All should be made to share alike in a feast.

396. A truly proper use for money is that of giving for the funeral expenses of the poor. One should sacrifice one's money for the salvation of the poor. One should send help to the homes of those who depend on unasked for help. 397. He who protects the poor, blind, lame and dumb, his wealth fulfils its true purpose. His good deeds are pure goodness.

398. The rich man who removes the distresses of *sādhus* and other good men, he has the banner of his righteousness raised in full view in Heaven. 399. The rich man who protects a *bhakta* of God, he pleases God, and in saving him He gives him the priority over other *bhaktas.*

400. He who offers his wealth at the feet of his *sadguru,* feet that are full of blessing, and the highest beneficence, 401. the banner of his righteousness is planted in the Heaven-of-Righteousness [*satyaloka*], and throughout all Vaikuṇṭha [Heaven of Vishṇu] and Kailās [Heaven of Śiva]; drums and banners proclaim him. 402. When one offers to his *sadguru* wealth righteously acquired, in that act there is the absence of selfish desire, and he is indeed a purified one. 403. He who with growing, increasing devotion to God, offers his wealth to his *guru,* the Husband-of-Lakshmi [Krishṇa] accepts him, and gives him His own special *bhakti.* 404. He who gives undivided *bhakti* to his *guru,* at his door stand the Fourfold-Deliverances [*moksha*] for the purpose of serving him, and the glorious Lord is not far from him. 405. He who offers his all, his body, his mind and his wealth at the feet of his *guru* will never, to the end of Time, experience the illusory fears of this worldly existence.. 406. Thus those who spend in this way the wealth that fortune may have brought to them, they attain the Supreme-Spiritual-Riches [*paramārtha*] through their wealth, and obtain happiness through their devotion.

407. Those who do not spend their money in this way, who are a pest to their own caste and family, and them-

selves will not properly eat, their wealth is but a heap of buried treasure. 408. Thus he who is miserly towards his own self, and his wealth is simply buried treasure, his wealth becomes the reason for his fall into Hell. The sorrows of the luster after wealth are very grievous."

409. And so the Miser said to himself, "I also, by this same attitude of mind have become a worthless wretch, through my buried treasures. The great wealth I had in my hands is now gone, and alas! alas! in deceiving myself I have lost my chance of Final Deliverance [*moksha*]. 410. In heaping up these buried treasures I have worked my own harm." Then in sorrow and deep agony he expresses his grief as follows:—

THE CONFESSION OF THE REPENTANT MISER.

411. "Neglecting the proper use of my wealth, and wasting away my body, speech and mind in straining efforts for the accumulating of riches, I became intoxicated and foolish. 412. And in this straining after riches my youth and strength, and life itself, have gone. My body is now altogether wasted away. I was not able to assuage my thirst for riches. 413. As I heaped up wealth on wealth I only increased my anxieties. Through it I forgot my true riches. Through my lust for riches I became a miser. 414. Those riches, through which by compassion to creatures, and by benefactions, men of sense, while even alive, have crossed safely the ocean of this worldly life, have been useless to me. 415. Unfortunate One! My wealth was accumulated in vain. My very existence has been in vain. My living has been in vain. My own true welfare has been

lost. 416. If I should now say, I being alive, I will accomplish my highest good, that thought is now of no avail, for both wealth and power have disappeared. 417. My wealth was spent in wrong doing, and old age has deprived me of strength. I am nothing now, but a decrepit old man, living, but smitten by ill fortune. 418. Alas! Alas! In acquiring wealth I robbed all other men." Realizing this now, the Miser thus tells his tale.

THE REPENTANT MISER REFLECTS ON THE SEDUCTIONS OF WEALTH.

419. "This is not merely true of the Ignorant. Even those who say that wealth is an evil, they also become eager for wealth. Even the wisest of men become crazy after wealth. 420. The Wise, thus made crazy, make continually both right and wrong efforts after wealth. 421. The cause for this craze of the Wise is wholly the *Māyā* of God, the characteristic of which is that it does the impossible, and so seduces the wise man. 422. But you will say that it is not the Māyā of Krishṇa by which a paṇḍit is seduced, but rather that he (by his own will,) acquires wealth for his own happiness, and through his desire for enjoyment. 423. Moreover those who say that happiness comes through the selfish use of wealth, are also fools." The Miser further explains his reasoned thoughts on this point, as follows:—

NO TRUE ENJOYMENT IN MERE RICHES.

424. "Alas! Alas! The Twice-born, who through superiority of birth is worshipped, even he may be seduced by the seductions of Māyā. The body that he nourishes, in his selfish use of wealth, is perishable. 425. The various

selfish enjoyments of the body become its wasting disease. Gathering much riches is the very path to the loss of riches. 426 . Because wealth comes to him without effort, the rich man seeks for it. If he had to toil hard in accumulating it, where would be the enjoyment he gets from his desires of it? 427. Thinking there is happiness to be found in intercourse with women, one keeps a woman for his happiness, but she in many ways becomes an irritation, from which he is unable to free himself, though through bitter tears. 428. If the thought is to give one's body happiness through wife, son, fulfilments of desires, and enjoyments, still that body is always at the point of death, and Death is close upon him. 429. As the hours of one's life go by, age destroys them. Where then is the sweetness of the enjoyment of them, yet the desire for wealth makes even wise men foolish. 430.* A frog may be eating a fly, while passing down the mouth of a serpent. The enjoyment in eating that fly does not free him from the grasp of the serpent, as one can truly understand. 431. So the death of the body is not prevented through the many enjoyments given to it. Yet knowing this, the Wise even become blind through the desire for wealth. 432. Although a doer, yet he is subject to the law of death. What enjoyment can then bring him comfort? This is the very confusion that Māyā brings about. Some of the greatest *sādhus* have been seduced by it. 433. Even if by wealth one gained Heaven in the next life, the enjoyment of it would still be painful, for when the enjoyment is finished, the fool, who has depended on his acts, has to fall into Hell. 434. Even after doing the acts that

---

*Taken from Dnyāneśvari 13 :731.

are enjoyable and desirable, yet there is before one death and birth again, to be forever experienced. This pain in its intensity belongs to the one who lusts for wealth. 435. I certainly experienced no joy from the lust for wealth. I was also a fool of that very kind. But now by my good fortune I have lost my wealth."

THE REPENTANT MISER REGARDS HIS LOSS OF WEALTH AS A BLESSING.

436. "It was formerly that I was really most unfortunate. Now I have become most fortunate. Śri Raṅga [Krishṇa] is pleased with me. I have come to right-thinking [*Viveka*] and to the discarding of worldly things [*Vairāgya*]. 437. My accumulation of wealth was the chief cause of my lack of knowledge. Hari has taken it away. By this he has shown me his rich favor. 438. He takes away [*hari*] the ignorance of His *bhaktas,* therefore, he is named Hari. By manifesting His full favor to me, He has brought my mind to its right thinking. 439. The Discarding of worldly-things [*Vairāgya*] without Right-Thinking [*Viveka*] is Blindness. Right-Thinking [*Viveka*] without the discarding of worldly things [*Vairāgya*] is Lameness. But in my heart the two have been conceived as twins, and born at the same time. 440. So Hari has had mercy on me, and taken away my wealth, which was my Ignorance, and made the two, Right-Thinking [*Viveka*] and the Discarding-of-worldly-things [*Vairāgya*], to shine in the province of my heart. 441. No one knows when, where, under what special circumstances, Hari shows such mercy. 442. In order to draw away the heart of His *bhakta* from riches, He may take those riches away. And

making their hearts good, through the removal of their riches, may give them *vairāgya* and *viveka.* 443. His skill in giving and taking away is quite beyond the understanding even of Brahmadeva and the other Gods, therefore He is blessed; to whom the six-qualities are subject. 444. Although He is unthinkable and infinite, yet to me He has become merciful, and destroying my sin, together with my wealth, has lighted for me the lamp of Knowledge. 445. Because God has shown this mercy towards me, those Presiding Goddesses of the Five Sacrifices, who destroy when angry, will not destroy me. 446. For he who has Hari as his protector, who holds the brilliant disk in his hand, no wind of opposition can blow upon him, and the gods praise him."

LOSS OF WEALTH A SIGN OF GOD'S MERCY.

447. "The Gods respectfully saluting Pralhāda, calmed Nṛisinha. He whom Narahari [God] protects, how can opposition prevail against him? 448. He who in a moment's time freed scores of gods from imprisonment, how could some inferior god even bend a hair of one of His *bhaktas.* 449. If God, who holds all gods in his control, whose feet the gods worship with bowed heads, if He is one's helper, no opposition can ever harm one. 450. He, through whose might the gods have come into power, He, whose parts the gods are, if He, Hari, is Himself pleased with one, how can there arise the opposition of anyone? 451. Śri Hari is the complex of all the gods. My Hari appears in the form of Indra and the Moon. So now as a poor man in this worldly-existence, there can be no longer any troubles for me. 452. As for the cause of this mercy towards me, it is not through any act of mine in this life,

it is an old former debt which God incurred. 453. Formerly, in some country, in some sacred watering place, or city, in some family line, I must have performed some good deed by which Hari was pleased. 454. And now having seen me in greatest suffering, Hari, full of mercy, is pleased with me. And it is through His mercy that I have come to my right-thinking. 455. Be it so that I have pain through the loss of my wealth, yet it is through that very pain that I have found my true joy. For see you, in order to sail safely over the ocean of this worldly life, the Discard-of-worldly-things [*Vairāgya*] and Right-Thinking [*Viveka*] form my staunch ship."

THE REPENTANT MISER SEEKS A WHOLLY SPIRITUAL LIFE.

456. Then overflowing with joy the Brahman said to himself, "Of the balance of my life I will not let so much as half a moment pass in vain. I will utterly destroy in me both joy and sorrow. 457. What care I now for the fears of this worldly-existence! I will take vengeance on the ten millions of rebirths. In my present body I am determined to make up fully for my hitherto spoiled life. 458. My body has arrived at full maturity, but my mind has not reached its old age. So thinking of God with that mind I will now break the bonds that fasten me to this worldly life. 459. With my remaining life I will break the teeth of this Kaliyuga. I will dig the grave of the pain of existence-in-the-womb. I will destroy Death itself. 460. This body, through which I have done both right and wrong, I will dry it up. By force of mental effort I will become one without consciousness of body. 461. My Enlightenment shall make an assault, and free my soul from

the imprisonment caused by my body. I will break the chain of joy and sorrow, and lift up the banner of Final-absorption-in-God [*sāyujyatā*]. 462. Now armed with Discard-of-worldly-things [*vairāgya*] and Right-Thinking [*viveka*], and awake to my highest good, as I go on seeking for the Supreme-Spiritual-Riches, they will gradually come to my hand. 463. There is no law that I alone can attain the Supreme-Spiritual-Riches [*paramārtha*]. Whoever is possessed with Discard-of-worldly-things [*vairāgya*] and Right-Thinking [*viveka*] the Supreme-Spiritual-Riches [*paramārtha*] are at his service. 464. The characteristic of this *Vairagya-viveka* is that though actually possessing wealth in the form of body, home, wife, and the like, the heart is not set upon it. This is the comprehensive meaning of *vairāgya*."

THE REPENTANT MISER PRAYS TO GOD FOR HELP.

465. "And now at this beginning of my new life, O God of Gods, together with all the multitudes of gods and goddesses, be my helpers, I pray you! 466. O Divinities, presiding over the senses, be all of you my helpers. In order that I may attain the Supreme-Spiritual-Riches [*paramārtha*] give me victory over my senses. 467. If God, the acknowledged Lord of the universe, is my helper, the divinities will all of them help me also, being as they are but Hari in forms pervaded by Him. 468. Considering Hari as in the form of divinities, I will serve all the divinities. So as helper in the salvation of the needy, may He save me in the ocean of this worldly-existence.

469. One may say to me, "You have come to the end of your life. You are now merely a decrepit old man. Why do you in vain take all this trouble in your old age?" 470. Do not think of me thus. The famous Khatvāṅga attained in a moment the Supreme-Spiritual-Riches, receiving his highest good. 471. What if I have a much longer life than he had. If the gods help me, I shall attain the Supreme-Spiritual-Riches [*paramārtha*] also in the twinkling of an eye. 472. If the *viveka-vairāgya*, which I now have to-day, remains with me, and is used, then what indeed can poor Kaliyuga do! I shall have conquered this worldly-existence."

KRISHṆA RELATES THE CHANGE IN THE REPENTANT MISER.

473. Krishṇa relates the remarkable story of what the miser formerly was, and how his character changed in becoming possessed with *viveka* and *vairāgya.*

474. "That Brahman of Avanti, who was a most miserly man, lost all the property he had, and became changed into one who discarded all worldly desires. 475. If one has in his mind *vairāgya* and *viveka* the attainment-of-Brahma is at his service." All this was told by Krishṇa to Uddhava for the purpose of helping him to realize his true spiritual self. 476. Formerly that Brahman miser was of low character, avaricious, and a doer of contemptuous deeds. The same man has now become a most excellent Twice-born, a supreme *vairāgi,* through his *viveka.*

THE REPENTANT MISER DECIDES TO BECOME A SANNYĀSI.

477. "The determination, which I have already made, I will carry to its conclusion." said the miser. Such a seeker after the Supreme-Spiritual-Riches had the miser now become in the fulness of his joy. 478. "I myself was the cause of my sorrow. It was because I was possessed with the desire, lust and pride of riches that my distress has been so intense. 479. But my wealth has departed, leaving me sorrow behind. Wealth is, in fact, a vessel that contains sorrow. I, who was a luster after wife, son, and wealth, have been driven away by these very ones. 480. One ought to be proud of one's caste, but it is my very caste-fellows who have dropped me. All of my own folk have turned against me. Why now lust any more after them! 481. The chief cause of my lusting after wife, son, kin, and riches, was my desire for self-gratification. To all these I now make my final obeisance. 482. I make my final bow to my wife, children, friends and riches. My final bow to my caste and to all who belong to me. I make my final bow to self-gratification. There is now no further connection between you and me. 483. The reflection of the moon seems to dwell in the water, but the moon is distinct from the water, yet even so close a relation as that I have no longer with you. 484. Just as a shadow is ever and always bound to a solid substance, but that substance does not belong to the shadow, so now I have no connection with you. 485. Just as the youthful age comes to one's body, and youthfulness comes in its superabundance, yet finally it deserts the body, so I desert you. 486. The Spring-time enters a forest, and the glorious forest breaks

out into beauty. But as the Spring-time leaves the forest, so I leave the thoughts of myself and of mine. 487. Oh, the greatness of *vairāgya* and *viveka* that has caused in me this extraordinary revulsion against worldly things. I make therefore my Til-water funeral offering to Self-Gratification and to the Idea of Possession."

THE REPENTANT MISER BECOMES A TRUE SANNYĀSI.

488. Just as for a cast-off son, a father, in the ceremony of breaking the jar, cuts off relation with him, so casting aside all pride of self he became a *sannyāsi,* 489. just as when a fruit has become overripe, it drops connection with the body from which it was born, the stem no longer holding the fruit, and the fruit no longer holding on to the stem, 490. So he no longer held on to pride of self; and pride of self, ashamed, would not come near him. In the purity of his feelings he would not so much as touch self-gratification. 491. As a lotus leaf, which although in the water, yet is not wet with the water, so only when untouched by self-gratification can one enter rightly into the order of the *sannyāsi.*

492. Other *sannyāsis,* while offering the burnt sacrifice, say "Anger and desire are burned away." But when the *til* seeds and *ghi* in the sacrifice are burned away, anger and desire are still there. 493. But such was not the character of this *sannyāsi's* sacrifice. All tendencies to wrong thinking were burned up. He made a complete burnt offering of anger and desire, together with all pride. 494. Having thus made a burnt sacrifice of his (evil) tendencies, he became a Three-staff-*sannyāsi.* And then, obtain-

ing permission from his *guru*, he began with joy his carefree wanderings.

THE REPENTANT MISER WANDERS AS A SANNYĀSI.

495. With conquered mind and vital airs, putting aside pride and the desire for praise, he wandered over the country in the fulness of supreme joy. 496. He who has no affection for his own body, what wish could he have for the society of others? So he wandered alone over the country, and in his enlightenment he was conscious only of his soul. 497. He lived always in a forest. Only for begging food did he ever enter a city. In towns where markets were held, he would beg, accepting whatever was given him. 498. He made no rule of going anywhere regularly to beg. On the contrary, he would appear unexpectedly, and be content with whatever he received. 499. Nor did he make it his rule to be a five or seven-house visitor. He had no pride whatever of any kind. 500. He did not bathe himself thoroughly. He simply dipped himself in water. Because of this he seemed of dark complexion. It was his purpose to look like an *Avadhuta* [Wandering *sannyāsi*] in appearance.

THE REPENTANT MISER APPEARS AT AVANTI AS A SANNYĀSI.

501. Thus wandering over the country he suddenly appeared at Avanti, now a very old man, a *sannyāsi,* in the garb of an Avadhuta [wandering *sannyāsi*]. 502. According to a custom prescribed by the *Achārya,* anyone entering the order of the *sannyāsi,* should at least once visit his old home.

THE HOSTILE RECEPTION OF THE SANNYĀSI.

503. When the people of the town saw him they exclaimed, "Hallo! That Brahman, who lost his property has become a *sannyāsi.*" 504. Hearing this, some of the very bad people gathered around him. Making signs to one another, they began a series of persecutions. 505. Although they troubled him a great deal, still not for a moment did his feelings experience a change. He felt no anger whatever, because of his Right-thinking [*vivekatā*] and complete self-control.

KRISHṆA PRAISES THE CALMNESS OF THE SANNYĀSI.

506. "I [Krishṇa] will give you examples of how the bad men troubled him, and the calmness with which he bore all. Listen with attention. 507. And if any hearer will fix his attention on what it illustrates, his Right-thinking will make him a wise man. And if he can grasp its true meaning in sincerity, he also will surely attain the same calmness of mind. 508. O Uddhava, you Moon, to whom the *chakora* bird of Reasoning looks up; you of pure character through the good fortune of being a devotee of God. You an Indra among men, with the good fortune of a calm mind, listen, you fortunate one! 509. In order that he might control his peace of mind, Krishṇa called to Uddhava, and thus awakening his attention said, "Such is the characteristic of peace of mind [*shanti*]. 510. He who never comes to the point of anger when his mode of living is opposed, or when insulted under the guise of

being honored, he indeed possesses this peace [*shanti*] of mind. Listen.

THE SANNYĀSI IS MALTREATED.

511. Bad people surrounded the *sannyāsi,* and thinking to irritate him fell at his feet. As they bowed, they all touched his feet. 512. One said, "He is an old *sannyāsi*" Another asked, "For how many years have you been a *sannyāsi*?" One demanded the rules of his order, and what *guru* had shaved his head. 513. One made a sign to another to ask him where his former home was. And another made a sign to ask him about his hoards of money. 514. So one said to him, "O *svāmi,* where was your former home? Were you a shopkeeper or a peddler? In what town did you live?" 515. Another said, "He has some money." A third, "No, he is now without money." Again another, "Don't trouble him. He is a *sannyāsi,* who has wholly discarded worldly-desires."

THE SANNYĀSI PRESERVES UNRUFFLED CALMNESS.

516. Although thus persecuted, the *sannyāsi* showed no irritation. He restrained himself in silence, not uttering a word. 517. Then said one, "The reason why he is a Three-staff-*sannyāsi,* is because formerly he was immensely rich. He has probably hollowed out his staves and filled them with money. This is the meaning of his being a Three-staff-*sannyāsi*". 518. One said, "He has had a great thousand-thread blanket made". To which another added, "And he has filled it full of money". 519. One remarked "Why do you look into his face? He has started a heresy". Thus they grossly insulted him. One snatched away his

three staves. 520 Another snatched away his begging bowl; another, his holy mat; another, his rosary; another, his yellow robe. 521. One declared, "He is one of my debtors. Luckily I have found him here." And with this remark he snatched away his blanket, taking with it even his loin cloth. 522. Yet, although these evil men did these things to him, yet his heart was not ruffled. He uttered not a word. His courageous heart was full of forgiveness. 523. He said to himself, "Both, one's going and coming, are entirely in the hands of the Unseen". Therefore, not taking any further trouble to beg for anything, the *sannyāsi* started to go away. 524. Seeing the *sannyāsi* departing, those knaves feigning politness prostrated themselves before him, and addressed him with the greatest show of humility. 525. "Hara!" "Hara" they exclaimed, "A great wrong has been done you. These boors, in their ignorance, do not differentiate between the worthy and the unworthy. 526. O *Svāmi,* do not let your heart hold any anger. Please accept these garments". And by falling at his feet they made him return that they might irritate him further to the utmost. 527. Thus to bring back the *sannyāsi* by a show of politeness, they put before him his staves and begging bowl, and others gave back his garments. Yet others again snatched them away. 528. Some remarked, "The *sannyāsi* is an old man. One should give him his garments." Another remarked, "To beat this rogue would be for us an act of greatest goodness." 529. When, instead of returning his garments to him, they ridiculed him, the *sannyāsi* started slowly to go away. Then some one had him return, and gave him his garments, saying, "Now you may go." 530. Then one ran towards him, beating him on his head, and snatching away his garments came back. "O give them back to him", cried another "Why do you trouble an old man so needlessly?" 531. On this the *sannyāsi* went away, leaving his garments behind. Then performing his bath and devotions, he started to beg for his food.

INSULTS TO MAKE THE SANNYĀSI TALK, CONTINUE.

532. After he had finished his begging, and dividing what he had received according to scriptural rites, he sat by the river bank to eat. The bad people, seeing him there, crowded around him. 533. "Hallo!" they cried, "He is not truly a *sannyāsi.* Why! He is the miser of our town. He does not say, Yes or No to this. This is his method of roguery. 534. Any one who fails to make him talk let him be his bastard son." With an oath that they would make him talk, they crowded around him. 535. One boasted "It won't take a moment for me to bring to naught his vow of silence. I know a way of making him yell aloud." 536. And so this great sinner, this most evil minded man, poured filth on the *sannyāsi's* head, as he was eating. And still no anger came to his heart. He remained cool in his state of soul-consciousness. 537. Then some said, "If one has anger in one's heart, one has thereby lost his calmness, even if he does not show it outwardly in his speech. If he does not talk, it is because he is ashamed before public opinion, or fearful, lest it interfere with his demands for food." 538. But that was not true of this *sannyāsi.* All thought of being ashamed of his acts had been washed away. His state of calmness was such that Anger could not ruffle it. 539. To be one thing within, another without, that is the chief characteristic of a hypocrite. Such was not the case with this *sannyāsi.* Within

and without his calmness was genuinely pure. 540. Those evil men now said, "See here! He absolutely refuses to talk". So they spat into his face, grossly insulting him. 541. Some said "Kick him." Some gave him a blow on his head. Still others said, "Let us not cease until we make him talk." 542. Some, who were standing at a distance, pierced the *sannyāsi's* heart with their word-arrows. "We know the real meaning of his yellow robe", they cried. 543. The purpose of his robe is to cover his great roguery, his evil deeds and hypocrisy. Under the guise of a mendicant, he is a wandering spy. Seize him! He is a real thief." 544. Thus they shouted out cries of evil accusation. One cried, "Bind him, bind him!" And some one did tie his two hands together with a strong cord, and fastened his head downwards. 545. Those who knew his former life, heaped insults upon him. "He was known as a miser", they cried, "and now he is exhibiting himself to us as a *sannyāsi*. 546. He heaped up riches by means both good and foul. That wealth vanished in wrong doing. His own people drove him away, and he was no longer able to obtain food. 547. So in order to obtain food now he is wearing the false guise of a *sannyāsi*. This shameless fellow has no shame. He is only putting on for us an appearance of worthiness. 548. He was formerly a deceiver, now he is a hypocritical *sannyāsi*. He thinks these are simple minded people who will not recognize his purpose. The great mute rascal! 549. As one puts on various guises in a comic show, so now he is a *sannyāsi* in a pious garb. But he is here to cheat us. Any one who beats him incurs no blame. 550. He is a great one among hypocrites! He remains firm to the guise he has assumed. Although we pester him, he is unmoved; as unmoved as Mount Meru, when attacked by a swarm of locusts. 551. The wisdom of his attitude of bravery is for the purpose of gaining food and clothing. This is why he has adopted the vow of silence, like the crane, planning his selfish interests. 552. Just as a crane adopts silence in order to catch and swallow a fish, so we must think of him. He does it to deceive the simple minded people. 553. Because of his lust for riches he does not bring to mind the former troubles he endured. It has become a fixed habit with him, hence he does not take notice of any trouble inflicted on him." 554. One exclaimed "He is self-control in visible form" and with that he began to kick him. One ran a straw up his nostril, saying, "Come now, let us watch his calmness." 555. Thus they pestered him, and made fun of him in many ways. Still no anger arose in his heart. He was unmoved in his calmness. 556. And the more they saw of his calmness, the more those evil people were angrily excited against him. They maltreated him in various ways. How they did so Shripati [Krishṇa] continues to describe as follows:—

557. "Perfect calmness has entered the heart of this miser", jestingly laughed one. Then one daubed his nose with lime. Another marked his face with lampblack. 558. One cried, "He is truly a great rogue", and with that he turned his back to him and made him a mock reverence. 559. And yet such was his composure that not the least anger came into his heart. Surely he is a true *sannyāsi* in all the three-worlds whose calmness of mind is unruffled even under such attempts to ruffle it. 560. Seeing that they could not make him angry, those evil people were stirred to greater anger themselves. They fastened a chain around his neck, and brought him bound to the public square. 561. "Recognize him, any of you. This is that miser,

that evil doer. We have found him here today, a great rogue, a hypocrite!" they cried. 562. They tied him with a rope, just as a juggler ties a monkey, and then gathering around him on all sides they pulled him back and forth. 563. One pulled him to the East, another to the West, the *sannyāsi* in the meanwhile smiling to himself, thinking how all these people were getting pleasure out of their treatment of him. 564. "My body is experiencing the results of deeds done in a former birth. What relation has that to Me!" With this thought in mind he forgave them fully, and would do nothing in return to irritate any of them. 565. He who will suffer insults without irritation in the presence of those of one's own caste, one's own relatives and friends, who formerly may have greatly respected him. 566. Such an one possesses indeed perfect calmness. Know this for certainty, O Uddhava. But he who would feel ashamed of being treated so, because of his desire for public praise, such an one has not true calmness of mind. 567. Thus while they attempted to stir him to anger, his feelings were not stirred up." What the *sannyāsi* thought, the God of gods relates as follows:—

THE SANNYĀSI REASONS ON HIS SUFFERINGS.

568. The *sannyāsi* reasoned thus to himself. "Mankind is bound by the three forms of *prārabdha.* It is absolutely necessary for us to have the experience of them. Neither prince nor pauper can free themselves from them. 569. The sufferings that come to us from the acts of created beings may be called Creature-caused sufferings. Those that come from divinities may be called Divinity-caused sufferings. Those that take place in the body, like

fever for example, may be called Physically-caused sufferings. 570. Thus *Prārabdha* becomes the cause of three kinds of suffering. While suffering them one feels it grievous, but this is pure foolishness, arising from the dullness of one's intellect. 571. The sufferings which come from *prārabdha* cannot be avoided by mankind, even if Hara [Śiva] or Hari [Vishṇu] are made our helpers. Understanding this law, the *sannyāsi* showed a forgiving spirit. 572. Although Krishṇa was the helper of the Pāndavas, still they met with misfortunes. Though one makes Hara or Hari one's helpers, *prārabdha* cannot be escaped.

573. So although maltreated by those evil people, the *sannyāsi* did not lose his calmness of mind. He controlled himself with noble determination, and his righteous state of mind was unshaken. 574. In the midst of this persecution the mendicant sang a song. I will repeat it to you, O Uddhava. Listen very attentively to its teachings. 575. If one takes to heart the lesson of that song, Duality resolves itself into Unity, the joy of calmness comes naturally, and final Release-from-bondage comes to his home." 576. It was Uddhava's good fortune, the best in the world, that Krishṇa should bring this song to his attention. Listen to the strains of the Mendicant's Song.

THE MANA [MIND]* IS THE CAUSE OF JOY AND SORROW.

577. The three kinds of men, the very good, the very bad, and the ordinary, are not at all the cause of my happiness or sorrow. 578. Men, as many as there are, are

*Mana is the organ [*indriya*] of thought, imagination, willing and memory.

formed of the five-elements. My own body is made up of the same five elements. I am, therefore, by nature one and the same with them. Happiness and sorrow belong to the *mana* [mind as organ of imagination).

579. If one contends that the givers of happiness or sorrow are divinities, those divinities are merely a conception of the *mana.* The happiness or sorrow they cause do not touch Me. 580. The *mana* is a divinity in form, and it is the *mana* that has conceived the host of divinities. So the happiness or sorrow that they may give has their chief cause in the *mana* itself. 581. According to one's mental [*mana*] conception, gods and goddesses appear in some form or other. Where the *mana* forms a wrong conception, there even a god that may exist is unperceived. 582. Therefore all divinities are *mana*-conceived. So that all the responsibility for happiness or sorrow, that comes from them, rests on the head of the *mana* [mind as organ of imagination].

583. That the *ātmā* [soul] is the cause of happiness and sorrow is absolutely false. The *ātmā* has absolutely no duality connected with it. 584. "I, *Atma,* am a giver of happiness and sorrow, or he, an *Ātmā,* is a partaker of joy and sorrow". This can never be said by the *Ātmā.*

585. The malignant planet, under which one was born, is assumed by some to be the cause of joy and sorrow. But the *mana* is the planet of the planets, and therefore it is the *mana* that causes birth and death. 586. The revolutions of the planets are only as long as our body lasts. The movements of the *mana* are of a nature superior to them. The *mana* causes many kinds of sufferings, that from births to births never leave one. 587. An evil planet may cause

us evil for a short time, but the evil caused by the *mana* extends over ten millions of births. The evil planet after causing evil, desists, but the *mana* never leaves one even to the end of Time. 588. If the *mana* does not possess the consciousness of body, it can then have no idea of evil caused by a planet. Therefore, know certainly that the cause of joy and sorrow is that planet, the *mana* itself.

589. If one should affirm that it is one's own *karma* that is the cause of sorrow, this cannot be maintained. *Karma* is the very thing that delivers one from the bondage of *karma*. How then can it be the giver of sorrow? 590. The natural functioning of one's *karma* is pure. It is the *mana* that makes one do these natural acts with desire, and so makes one suffer many sorrows during many births. 591. But let us assume that they do take place by the action of *karma*. Then it is to be affirmed that as the conceptions of the *mana* do not affect *karma*, one's own *karma* quickly gets rid of one's many joys and sorrows. 592. This body does not feel joy or sorrow. The *Ātmā* also has absolutely no knowledge of joy or sorrow. It is the *mana* through its own peculiar nature, that provides the cart-loads of joy and sorrow. 593. So that the sole cause of joy and sorrow is the *mana*, and mankind being in its power, feels the joys and sorrows that are really illusory.

594. That Kāla [Time, Death] is the giver of joy and sorrow, cannot at all be maintained, for the power of *Kāla* is but a *mana-conceived* idea. 595. Although the I [the *Ātmā*] is without old age and death, the *mana* conceives the idea "I am liable to death." From that moment one feels that Death is constantly after one, to destroy one. 596. For example, one has stuck a needle in his bedding

with his own hand. At night it happens to prick his hand, and he dies from the fear that a serpent has bitten him. 597. But a serpent had not really bitten him. How then did he get poisoned? He died because of his imagination. Just so Death comes to men. 598. Take another example. A serpent attacked a man's back. "What has pierced me"? He says to his companion, "Tell me." The other replies "I wonder how you were pierced by a thorn. I have easily pulled it out, however." 599. He had no idea that it was a serpent that had bitten him, and so the poison did not spread. He continued happily his occupation. 600. But after some time some one pointed out to him the marks of the bite, and reminded him of the snake. Immediately the poison spread through him, and he died, because of his imagination. 601. Thus when to a person who is free from doubt there arises a doubt regarding his good thoughts, then Kāla girds his loins for his destruction. 602. He, whose *mana* sincerely says with certainty, "I am immortal," Kāla turns away from his house. Death, hard to bear, comes from the conception of the *mana*. 603. He who is truly free from doubt, *Kāla* never comes to him. There is nothing perishable before him, so where will *Kāla* find an entrance? 604. Thus one sees that *Kāla* is not the giver of joy and sorrow. The begetter of joy and sorrow is in truth the *mana*. 605. This worldly existence [*samsāra*] is a conception of the *mana*. Birth and death have been imagined by the *mana*. It is the *mana* that causes the coming and going, again and again, into and from this worldly-existence [*samsāra*].

606. The above six catagories are reputed to be the causes of joy and sorrow, but when examined, this is seen

to be without proof. Joy and sorrow are begotten of the *mana.* 607. Notice how strangely the *mana* acts. Intelligence creates the idea of I, and making the I a living personality, causes it to feel joy and sorrow. 608. The mote in the eye is small, but it gives the body intense pain. So the *mana,* by its possession of mere desire, causes intensity of joy and sorrow.

609. But you may say, that in this case it is Ignorance that is the cause of joy and sorrow. But since Ignorance is itself Brahma, neither joy nor sorrow can arise without the *mana.* 610. Ignorance being Brahma, the *mana* in dreamless sleep is unconscious, so that in that state there is neither joy nor sorow. No one has ever felt them in that state. 611. When the *mana* is unconscious, the feelings which the body possesses are not felt as joy or sorrow. They are only seen to exist in the body. 612. Therefore, the cause of joy and sorrow lies in the *mana* itself. The *mana,* causing birth and death, creates the hard-to-bear revolutions of the wheel of this worldly-existence."

THE SANNYĀSI EXPLAINS THE CHARACTERISTICS OF THE *MANA.*

613. In what way the *mana* involves one in the whirlpool of this worldly existence, the Mendicant himself explains.

614. "The *mana,* through its power of imagination, creates various feelings. These have a triple nature. The character of these feelings depend on the proportion in which they contain the three *guṇas.* [qualities]. 615. The mana, having created the three worlds with the various classes of beings, gods, men, beasts, birds and the like, and

with their varying proportions of the three *gunas,* acts on the plane of this worldly-existence. 616. The might of the *mana* is extraordinary. It builds up its creations in a moment, and destroys them in a moment. The *mana* causes illusions even to Brahmadeva and the other gods. Then what can be expected of poor inferior beings. 617. See what the power of the *mana* is! It catches in the snare of the *guṇas,* the *Nirguṇ* [Brahma] Itself, and giving It the dream of being a living being, makes It whirl in the revolutions of the wheel of *samsāra.* 618. If one seeks to characterize the *Mana,* it is in itself inanimate, without understanding and without intelligence." How is it created? The Mendicant explains as follows :—

HOW THE MANA IS CREATED.

619. The *Ātmā* is in the form of pure intelligence. It is unassociated, unchangeable, and without qualities [*nirguṇ*]. I can, therefore, never be involved in the bondage of worldly-existence [*samsāra*]. 620. That which is a mass of light through its own light; that which is brilliant through its own refulgence, this pure, supreme *Ātmā* cannot have action and conduct ascribed to it. 621. And certainly when one thinks of the *mana* as an inanimate conjunct, it also cannot experience *samsāra.* How then does bondage to the worldly-existence take place? Listen. 622. The peculiarity of the *mana* is most strange. To pure Intelligence it brings the consciousness of I. That brings to that Being the conception of being a living personality, which in turn brings to it the conception that it possesses qualities [*guṇas*]. 623. The power of the *mana* is such that it makes of the pure the impure, and forming a three-*guṇa*

garland binds with it the knot of bondage to this worldly-existence [*samsāra*]. 624. Just as the portion of water in the water-vessel contains the orb of the moon, but without the moon being affected thereby, so the *Ātmā,* as pure Intelligence is made complex merely by the misconception of the *mana.* 625. By shaking the water in the vessel, the moon is made to vibrate. So is the idea of birth and death for the pure *Ātmā.* Joy and sorrow are caused by the *mana.* 626. The *Ātmā* is self-illuminating in the form of Intelligence. The *mana* is inanimate, and in the form of imagination. The *Ātmā,* thinking it has the same form as the *mana,* experiences the right and the wrong doing of the *mana.*

627. The One Supreme *Ātmā* is truly the relative, the friend, the close kin of every living being [*jiva*]. He is the ruler of the *mana* and of the living being [*jiva*], and the Witnesser, through His function of witnessing. 628. The *Ātmā,* as seen reflected in Ignorance, forming thereby the individual life [*jiva*] is my close kin. But confused by the misunderstandings of the *mana,* He feels the *mana*-begotten joys and sorows. 629. The *mana's* association with the individual *Ātmā* [*jiva*] is very close. Through it the living being [*jiva*] falls into a great delusion. Although he is really a non-doer, he experiences the results of actions and of failures to act. 630. Primarily the individual soul [*jiva*] is the ruler of the *mana,* but because of the *mana's* oneness with it, it feels the joys and sorrows created by the *mana,* although they are really non-existent. 631. Just as when there is a very close relation between a Minister and a King, the Minister holds the King very strongly in bondage to himself. The consequence is that

the King has to be humble, and enjoy or suffer whatever joys or sorrows the Minister provides. 632. The same is the condition of the individual soul [*jiva*]. The *mana* has involved it in this worldly-existence, so that it has to suffer many births and deaths, and everlasting joys and sorrows. 633. If therefore the *mana* is not controlled, the individual [*jiva*] cannot escape sorrow. If one has to dance for the pleasure of the *mana,* all efforts to escape sorrow are in vain.

CONTROL OF THE MANA IS NECESSARY.

634. If one should pay no attention to the control of the *mana,* while giving away all one's possessions, a pride arises in the thought "I am a giver." Thus through that giving the *mana* becomes proud. 635. Though failing to realize the significance of the control of the *mana*, one may carry out fully the duties belonging to his caste, and his status in life [*āśrama*]. But thereby his *mana* tends to conceit and the thought comes 'My acts are the very noblest. 636. I am the only great one in all the Three-worlds. I have perfectly performed my duties. I am the cook of my own dinner." Thus through the very act of performing one's duties, the *mana* tends to become more conceited. 637. Where there is no will for controlling the *mana* the law of control works in an opposite way; so the man says to himself, "I am most certainly a *sādhu.*" This follows from the very law of the *mana.* 638. One listens to the reading of the *Vedas* and *shāstras,* and a full tide of pride comes in, pride in one's learning. Where is the control of the *mana* there? 639. One starts to perform his special duties. They may be very strict. Then there arises the illusion that one is a scrupulously exact doer. Where is there here the control

of the *mana*? 640. Actions belong only to the body. The *Ātmā,* though it is within a body, is really without a body. That it can be in the toils of *karma* is the foolish opinion of some strict orthodox. 641. A ritualist thinks to perform an infinite number of rites. He does this out of a wish for money and grain. Thus having no control of his *mana,* his good rites are performed in vain. 642. The control of the *mana* is the chief fruit of religious rites, of the act of giving, and of all forms of prescribed duties. Without this control all is incomplete, and the means the Seeker employs (for his salvation) are fruitless. 643. The seven acts, such as Giving and the like, are essentially connected with knowledge. How can one then say that these means are fruitless? 644. (The answer is) the fruits which result from the acts of giving and the like, belong to this life and the next. If that fruit is itself fruitless, it but increases births and deaths. 645. The Seeker [*Sādhaka*] becomes possessed of Knowledge by absolutely ridding himself of the desire for the fruit of knowledge. Giving, and the other performances of one's special duties, are useful for the purification of the heart. 646. But that my thought may be "I wish my heart to be pure," needs primarily the aid of God. Then the means employed will accomplish the desired end.

BHAKTI AS A MEANS FOR CONTROLLING THE MANA.

647. Amongst the means my *bhakti* is the chief. And in that the principal thing is repeating the names of God. Through his Name comes purity of thought to one's thinking, and the Seeker attains his proper spiritual state. 648.

There is no means that is more helpful than the Name of God. By that Name comes the cleaving of the bonds that bind to this worldly-existence. Know this most certainly, O Uddhava.

MEANS UNNECESSARY IF THE MANA IS NOT FUNCTIONING.

649. One is in one's true state when the *mana* is not functioning. Then all Means slink away in shame. Then the need of Giving and the like naturally cease to exist. 650. In the case where the *mana* of a man leaves its birth-place, what place can there be for Giving and the like among the Means. 651. If you pass even dainty food to a man who has satiated himself with food, just as he will not so much as smell it, just so is the employment of Means to one who has ceased to be dominated by his *mana*. 652. When a river is in high flood, one uses great effort in rafting across, but when the flood has subsided, one rejects the use of the raft altogether. 653. So when Desire and Anger and the like are without action, and his *mana* is not functioning in producing illusions, he certainly has no need for acts of Giving and the like. 654. Just as when after the sun has risen, there is no need for millions of lamps, so when the *mana* is not imagining, the millions of means are of no use. 655. So in the case of him whose *mana* has reached its perfect calmness, there is no need for him to perform those acts of Giving and the like, for all forms of thought have ceased to be. 656. But he, whose *mana* is uncontrolled, always irrational, and constantly attached to sensual things, to him also the Means [*sādhana*] are of no use. 657. Just as an army flees in twelve directions when facing an

assault of mad elephants, so the sensually inclined find that the Means are powerless. 658. He, whose *mana* is attached to sensual things, will not so much as even touch the Means of deliverance. But if he does, even in employing the Means he has sensual thoughts. 659. In employing the Means, [*sādhana*] it fructifies into whatever his heart desires; so that Giving and the like become of no account. 660. Just as when a feeble rider is on a fiery steed, he is powerless to restrain his horse, not a moment quiet. 661. So is he whose *mana* is very evil, and full of sensuous desires and anger, and who is under the power of that *mana,* and whose reason is drowned in sensual seductions. 662. What use could such an one make of the Means of Deliverance? What he does do, he does because he is seduced. By this his evil quality [*tamoguṇa*] is increased, and control of his *mana* becomes impossible. 663. If the senses, Hearing and the others, are forced into bondage, and the Means of Deliverance are employed, that does not subdue the *mana* for the senses are under the dominion of the *mana.*

THE MANA DOMINATES THE SENSES.

664. The *mana* controls every one, and no one can control the *mana.* The *mana* has made trouble even for the gods. How then can it come under the dominion of the physical senses? 665. The Moon is the divinity presiding over the *mana,* but the *mana* brought trouble to the Moon, by causing him to have adulterous relations with the wife of his *guru,* and as a punishment the Moon is attacked with wasting disease [Phases of the moon]. 666. Brahmadeva is the presiding divinity over the intellect, but it was the *mana* that corrupted the thoughts of Brahmadeva. Although his daughter repulsed him, yet he

carnally desired her. 667. It is over Thought that Vāsudeva presides. The *mana* surreptitiously deceived him, and causing him to fix his thought on Vrindā, made him fall into the cemetery. 668. Rudra is the presiding divinity over self-consciousness. The *mana* also deceived him. Carnally desiring the wife of the Rishi, the great Rishi cursed him. 669 Thus the *mana,* which is unconquerable even by the gods, how can it be controlled by any human being? If one affirms, therefore, that the senses rule the *mana,* it must be answered rather that the senses are in the power of the *mana.* 670. When the *mana* takes the senses in its grasp, and is fixed in its determination, the state of those senses is that they are entirely useless. 671. When there is the connection of the senses with the objects of sense, if the attitude of the *mana* is indifferent, the objects of the senses are not realized, for the senses lose their inspiration. 672. When following the law of the *mana,* there is no attachment to the objects of sense, the senses are unable to function, for the group of senses is in the control of the *mana.* It never occurs that the *mana* is ruled by the senses. 673. The *Mana* is the king of the senses. The senses do not function without the *mana.* The *mana* subdues the man himself. 674. Among all the powerful ones the *mana* is the most powerful. This being so, what can the poor senses do? For to restrain the *mana* even the superior beings have no power. 675. Kāla, in His might, seizes everything, but he cannot so much as pluck out a hair of *mana.* Even in acts of creation, preservation, and destruction, He cannot equal the *mana.* 676. The *mana* cannot be cut with a sword. Water cannot dissolve it. Fire cannot burn it. The ethereal space cannot turn it into vacuity. 677. Disease cannot attack the *mana*. There is no wasting sickness that can waste it away. When one looks to find some way of controlling the *mana*, one finds absolutely no way. 678. The *mana* creates scores of gods, such as Brahmadeva and others. The *mana* creates and destroys the universe. The *mana*, in the sweep of its imaginations, drives the Three-worlds into a wild dance. 679. The *mana* gives trouble to Kalikāla. The *mana* swallows the fire of the final destruction. The *mana* is the most powerful among all powers. There is nothing that can control the *mana*. 680. The *mana* is hard of control by the gods. The *mana* is most terrible of all terribles. The *mana* even controlled Hara and Hari. Who can stand up before the *mana*? 681. The blows of the *mana* are tremendous. Who can withstand the *mana*? There is no one to be seen among gods, men or demons who can conquer the *mana*. 682. There is no one sufficiently powerful in all the Three-worlds to wrestle with the *mana*. It is the *mana* that controls Kalikāla. It swallows the Rudra of the final Destruction, without so much as letting him touch its wisdom teeth. 683. Such being the infinite activity of the *mana*, it is called God. Such is the frightfulness of the *mana* that it is called Bhishmadeva, the horrible."

THE SANNYĀSI TELLS OF THE NEED OF A GURU TO CONTROL THE MANA.

684. "Such being the uncontrollable nature of the *mana* I will tell you the secret of how the *mana* can yet be controlled. Listen with attention. 685. Just as a diamond has to be cleaved by a diamond so the *mana* must be controlled

by the *mana.** And this only becomes possible when one has acquired the favor of a *guru.* 686. The *mana* is the serving maid of the *guru.* The *mana* is always in fear of a *sadguru.* If the *mana* is placed at the feet of the *sadguru,* the Seeker finds satisfaction.

687. There is one great truth relating to the *mana,* [the Will] that if it is itself inclined to acquire the Supreme-Spiritual-Riches, all the four forms of Deliverance become its slaves, and the Supreme-Brahma Itself is handed over to it, bound. 688. The *mana* is the *mana's* own light. The *mana* is the *mana's* own means to an end. The *mana.* is the *mana's* own hindrance. The *mana* is the destroyer of the *mana.* 689. As an illustration, the bamboo shoots increase the size of the bamboo cluster, but bamboo in friction with bamboo creates a spark and the cluster burns up. 690. So while the *mana* is planning death for the *mana,* it takes it to a *guru,* and trusting in his words, pays him reverence in all humility. 691. If the favor of the *Sadguru* is complete, the *mana* will manifest its intentions to the *mana,* and the *mana,* passing over to the *mana* its own joy, the *mana* becomes pleased with the *mana.* 692. When the *mana* becomes pleased with the *mana,* then the functions of the *mana* are without self-consciousness. Thus the *mana* makes it possible for the Seeker to possess himself in peace. 693. And having experienced a love for the favor of the *guru,* the *mana* quickly raises the banner of victory of *mana* over

---

*This in terms of Western psychology is the struggle of Good thoughts with Evil thoughts. The Good Mind can conquer the Evil Mind.

mana, and passes it over directly into the hands of the Seeker. 694. Thus the *mana* gives to the Seeker its own victory, and finally, when fully enlightened by the teachings of the *guru,* the *mana* realizes its own oneness with its own *Ātmā.* 695. As when a salt crystal falls in the ocean, it dissolves and become as large as the ocean. 696. So when the Seeker becomes unconscious of self, he becomes himself the whole Brahma, losing the idea of I and Thou. 697. When from his point of view he sees himself as the whole universe, the threefold dualities are swallowed up, and joy and sorrow can no longer affect him. 698. In that case how can there be joy? How can there be sorrow? How can there be bondage? How deliverance? How can there be a pandit? How a fool? The one Brahma is the one and all. 699. How can there be God or *bhakta*? Who can there be calm, and who disturbed? Duality and non-duality have in this case both disappeared. There remains The Absolute-Substance, alone, eternally in joy. 700. Doing and not-doing, both cease. Law and non-law melt away in shame. How can there be then the bad, the good, or the medium. Brahma alone fills all in all. 701. How can there be there either *shāstras* or *Vedas,* How can there be intellect or enlightenment? All differences have entirely disappeared. Supreme-Joy remains the all in all. 702. Such is victory over the *mana;* such the height that Faith can reach! God [Krishṇa] Himself describes this, and therefore, there can be no doubt about it. 703. The excellence of a victory over the *mana,* a thing difficult even for Brahmadeva and the other gods, if made one's own, one becomes God of gods through his own self-enlightenment. 704. He who conquering his *mana* attains Janardana [God] in this human life, is blessed, blessed in this three-world universe, and purifies the earth. 705. By him our ancestors are saved. By him whole family lines obtain deliverance. By him they become one with Brahma, having conquered their *manas.* 706. Victory over one's *mana* is so extremely powerful that perfect peace becomes one's purchased slave. The whirlpools of joys and sorrows disappear, touching not his *Ātmā* life." 707. Thus with feelings of pleasure Chakrapāṇi [Krishṇa] related to Uddhava the thoughts of the Mendicant, and exclaimed, "Blessed in the Three-worlds is the victory over the *mana.* 708. He who has conquered his own *mana,* how can I sufficiently praise him! Shall I say he has by it made me his slave? or wholly bought me? 709. My joy is through his obtaining joy. My constant satisfaction is the thought of his satisfaction. I, the Eternal One, dwell in him. I am great in the Three-worlds through him. 710. "I and he" are word formations that do not belong to us. In my internal thinking as to our oneness he is me in truth."

THE MANA REQUIRES GREAT EFFORT TO CONQUER THE MANA.

711. Victory over the *mana** makes this state possible; but one who has not conquered his *mana,* and yet becomes proud, through some victory over a common place enemy, against such the mendicant hurls his scorn. 712. "A strong enemy, belonging to this world, approaches. He can be conquered by diplomacy, by being bought off, or other means. 713. But this method does not, mind you, work with the *mana.* One may employ diplomatic methods,

*The Good mind conquering the Evil Mind.

but it will not listen. 714. If one should give the *mana* objects of sense, as a gift, yet it is not satisfied by such objects. By this it becomes even more truculent, and then who can restrain it? 715. The method of peaceful restraining efforts will not work with the *mana*. One should belabour the *mana*. But for this carnal weapons do not work, because the desire to be labour the *mana* does not arise in the *mana*. 716. For this reason it is most difficult to conquer this *mana*-enemy, who through births and deaths ever continues to attack us in their fulness of joys and sorrows. 717. In the case of some other kinds of enemies, if they cannot be restrained, one can at least run rapidly away from them, and take refuge in some fort, or castle, and find deliverance there. 718. But the whole Three-worlds is too small a place to make it possible to flee from the *mana*. If one should hide oneself in some place, difficult of approach, even there the *mana* will straightway force its way. 719. The generals commanding the troops of the *mana*, namely Desire, Anger and the like, are mighty heroes. Their blows are difficult to withstand. They cause to roll in the dust even those who are mighty. 720. Foreign enemies come from a distance, and it requires many days for them to come. But this *mana*-enemy is at one's very side, ever joined to us. 721. In one's sitting down, ones eating, in one's privacy, when praying, or when in contemplation, the attack from the *mana* comes suddenly, and in its enmity wholly conquers us. 722. The pain from a foreign enemy is small. The pest of the *mana* is great. It compels one to endure the whirlpool of births and deaths. 723. Foreign enemies are mortal, but the *mana* can oppose Death itself. Unless this enemy is conquered, the great sorrows of life cannot be escaped. 724.

Neither gods nor men can withstand the swift assaults of the *mana.* No one can conquer it even by the severest efforts. For this reason its unconquerableness is recognized. 725. He who does not conquer the *mana,* but because of conquering a foreign enemy becomes proud, is a great fool. 726. The *mana* has to be conquered by the *mana.* This has already been told you in a former *Shloka* as the only true method for the conquest of the *mana.*"

THE MANA CAN CONQUER THE MANA BY FRIENDSHIP.

727. If the *mana* cannot be conquered by way of making it an enemy, then by showing it friendship, one may make it happy through friendship. 728. The friendship of ordinary friends is manifested in acts of kindness, and in the return of kindness, and this through such things as give pleasure at one another's homes, and at special seasons. 729. Such is not the friendship of the *mana.* It shows kindness without kindness having been done it. It drives away all sorrow, and makes one live in a sea of joy. 730. Even in the very closest friendships of this common life of ours one tells the other of his special sorrows. The other cannot deliver him from them, and has to say, "I cannot help you". 731. But such is not the friendship of the *mana.* You seat it by your side, ready to listen to you. You tell it your sorrows, and it takes away the great evil of births and deaths. 732. If you have the fear of death in your heart; if there is the lust for gold or sensual things; if your shameless thoughts are not ashamed even when women scorn you. 733. If you covet your neighbour's wife, or your neighbour's wealth; If you have hatred or insulting

thoughts of others, which in a moment will cause you to suffer the terrors of Hell. 734. As you continue to tell the *mana* that you have no rest from the power of the lust for things, and that you have received to the limit the sorrows springing from thoughts due to Duality, and how you are unable to control the actions of your senses. 735. The *Mana* listens to all this, and then there surges up in you the utmost distaste [*vairāgya*] for worldly-things. It gathers for you the riches of Right thinking [*viveka*] and through it seeks to drive away your sorrows. 736. If you appoint a thief as the keeper of your treasures, he, mind you, will keep off any other thief. So if you make of your *mana* a friend, the *mana* will destroy the evil nature of the *mana*. 737. If you are living in wrong doing the *mana* can keep the *mana* away. The *mana* will itself administer an oath to speech that it shall not utter an untruth. 738. O, how supreme is the friendship of the *mana*, to burn up wholly *karma* and *akarma*, to supply one with the secret of pure thoughts, and bring to one's memory day and night the name of Hari. 739. "Śri Rāma, Jayarāma"! In these two syllables lie the destruction of the greatest sins. The *mana* does not neglect that name for a moment, and constantly repeats the name of Hari. 740. It decapitates Untruth, it skins Unrighteousness, it breaks the legs of Doubt, and causes relations with Desire to cease. 741. It destroys the habitation of wrong thought, it breaks the teeth of a worldly life, it cuts off all distrust, and causes the banner of trust to be lifted up. 742. Thus with a mature sense of trust, one will come to the feet of his *sadguru*, placing at his feet, with trust, his body, his *mana*, his possessions. 743. The characteristic of perfect trust being in listening to the *guru's* words, as the touch-stone changes iron into gold, so his heart becomes changed by them. 744. The *guru* may cease his teachings, but the contemplation of them by the *mana* does not cease, just as the insect by constant contemplation of the bumble-bee assumes its form. 745. He then looks upon a beautiful woman, or on riches, as filth. Insult, honor, pride, those faults of the *mana*, the *mana* itself destroys. 746. Blessed, blessed, is the friendship of the *mana*. Trusting to it fully, it will destroy births and deaths. It will make life without old age and death. 747. If one thus makes a friend of the *mana*, he will find it supremely kind. It will take one's life by the hand, and give it a plunge into the ocean of joy. 748. In that ocean the *mana*-characteristics of the *mana* disappear. The characteristics of the individual soul belonging to the individual soul melt away. The course of bondage and release come to an end, and the fears of this worldly-existence ebb away. 749. The friendship of the *mana* is of a nature that it kills its own kin. In fact, it itself dies in the very act of its friendly kindness. The *mana* is no deceiver in its friendly acts. 750. Although the *mana* is ready to serve one in its friendship, and always near one, yet sinful man rejects its friendship and makes his friends of common men.

THE MANA TO BE TREATED AS ENEMY OR FRIEND

751. So either making the *mana* an enemy, one should kill it, or making friendship with it, win the *mano* through the *mana*. If these two ways are found impossible, then the *mana* should be altogether discarded. 752. One should then not do what the *mana* tells him to do. One should not even take the *mana* by the hand. One should leave the

mana entirely alone with all one's heart and soul. 753. What the *mana* calls joy, one should necessarily reject. What the *mana* calls sorrow, should likewise be discarded. 754. He, who thus makes his *mana* indifferent (to both joy and sorrow), becomes *mana*-less and finds in so doing marvellous peace. 755. He, who, making his *mana* an enemy, friend or indifferent, does not conquer his *mana,* and so continuing to be conscious of body, his coming and going into this worldly life does not cease.

THE RELATION OF *ĀTMĀ* TO THE BODY

756. The *Ātmā* is without body, a mass of intelligence, But the *mana* thinks, "I possess a body," and with that idea of body comes the idea of I, My, births and deaths, joys and sorrows. 757. The *Ātmā* is ever free, without body, but in seeing itself one with the *mana,* though bodiless, says, "I possess a body", and finally regards the body as though it were the *Ātmā* itself. 758. It is the *mana* that says "I, the body", and through this there comes the fixed idea of consciousness of body. So the body becomes the I, and there follows the conception of I and My. 759. "I am the all pure *satchidānanda,* [Brahma]". This, one forgets; and instead, one says, "I am a *Vaishya* a *Shudra,* a *Kshatriya,* a Brahman, a fool, a wise man. 760. I am slim, I am bald, I am humpbacked, squinteyed, I am stout, big, clever." Ascribing to oneself these bodily qualities, which do not really belong to one, one makes a show of being a man. 761. A *sannyāsi,* for example, in his dreams sees himself as an outcaste, afraid to touch a Brahman. That indeed is the condition of the individual soul [*jiva*]. 762. In reality, however, Oneself is the Supreme *Âtmā,* without any differentiation in Itself.

*Yet it regards as real I, My, wife, child, wealth, evil men, good men, the medium men, in their threefold differences. 763. Thus regarding as true these differences, which arise from the idea of body and *Âtmā*, the intelligence of the individual soul [*jiva*] becomes absolutely blind. 764. As in the unreal actions in a dream, so in this *mana*-conceived worldly-existence, by considering it as real, the consciousness of body has become strongly fixed. 765. And this consciousness of body becoming strong, there follows again births, and again deaths, and the individual soul [*jiva*] in its confusion revolves on the wheel of this worldly-existence. 766. Just as the sledge hammer cannot smite the fire in the hot iron, yet because of the fire's association with the iron it receives the blows of the sledge hammer. 767. So the ever free and pure *Ātmā*, by gaining the consciousness of body, believes itself to be a personality [*jiva*] and consequently suffers births and deaths. 768. Just as the oilman's ox has its eyes blindfolded, as it turns the mill, so a man, blinded by a consciousness of body, revolves in the great whirlpool of this worldly existence. 769. And yet, while suffering births and deaths in utmost sorrow, still he does not throw aside his consciousness of body, which is what puts him into the darkness of blindness. 770. But *samsāra* [worldly-existence] whose sorrows have no limit, which cannot be crossed because of its great difficulties, and the horrors of which have to be endured, is *mana*-conceived." 771. The *mana*, therefore, is the cause of joy and sorrow, as has been explained in the eighth *shloka*. The mendicant in his discourse shows that it is an illusion that men and the like are the cause of sorrow.

---

* स्त्रजन of the text evidently a mistake for सज्जन

THE BODY NOT THE CAUSE OF JOY AND SORROW TO THE ĀTMĀ.

772. As one is born from his mother's [*janani*] womb, he is called *jana* [one born]. Such an one cannot ever be the cause of my joy or sorroy. 773. A man gives pain to another man, but what connection has that with my *Âtmā*? The *Ātmā* is bodiless and pure. The discomforts of joy and sorrow do not affect it. 774. A physical body can give pain to a physical body. Every physical body is made up of the five elements. But when their mutual oneness is recognized, there can be no joy or sorrow whatever. 775. Just as when you pour water into water, you do not give it pain. Or when you light a lamp with another lamp, that lamp does not suffer pain. 776. So when the earthly touches the earthly the *Ātmā* does not have any feelings of joy or sorrow. The *Ātmā* does not feel joy or sorrow. It has no contact with the body.

THE JIVA DOES NOT CAUSE JOY OR SORROW TO THE ĀTMĀ.

777. One may say perhaps that joy and sorrow come to *jiva* [the individual *ātmā*] because of its consciousness of body; or that it is the sufferer of the pain from a source different from itself. But when one looks for that source it is not to be seen. 778. One's tongue gets between one's teeth, and is suddenly fiercely bitten. On whom does one visit one's intense anger? 779. In the swoop of one's wrath is one to smash one's own teeth, or pull out one's own tongue? So, when one's oneness with the world is recognized, there can be no occasion for anger. 780. He who falls by the push of some one near him, boils with

anger against him, but he who himself slips and tumbles, he looks forward and backward in shame, but without anger, and slinks away. 781. So I, being creature, and sufferer, I am the giver of my own pain. Now as I am one with the world, with whom am I to get angry? 782. It is thus plain that the cause of my sorrow is not from man. But if you say it comes from the multitude of divinities, that also cannot be true.

DIVINITIES NOT THE CAUSE OF JOY OR SORROW TO THE ĀTMĀ.

783. Assume that a cause of sorrow is from the acts of the gods, but the gods have their abode in bodies. The *Ātmā*, in its essence, is without a body. 784. The gods preside over the activities of the senses belonging to the body. But the *Âtmā* is indivisible, unchangeable, and untouched by joy or sorrow. 785. The ground is naturally formless. A wall upon it is possessed of form. So the *Vastu* [The absolute Essence] is formless, but it is here that God appears, changeable in form, and as a presiding deity. 786. When the earthen wall falls to the ground it becomes one with it. So in the Qualitiless and Changeless One the senses find their oneness in the presiding deity. 787. The senses whether in one's own body, or those in another's, are one and the same, through their presiding deity. So it is God who feels the intensities of the joys and sorrows of the senses. 788. A hand slaps a face. Here Indra and Agni are the presiding deities. So it is really Indra who slaps Agni. The *Âtmā*, which is changeless remains outside the resulting pain. 789. Or supposing a mouth bites a hand. In this case it is Agni who has bitten

Indra. The *Âtmā* is untouched by the divinities of the senses, and joy and sorrow cannot touch it. 790. Another's mouth spits on one's own mouth. Both mouths are presided over by Agni. In this case who is to get angry with whom? For in the *Âtmā*-form there is nothing but itself. 791. Whether spittle or urine, they have their source in the body. They are the children of the body. So that which is of the body falls on the body. Now here who is to be angry with whom? 792. A mouth gives a kiss to another mouth. Here it is Agni who has kissed Agni. Who is to feel pride in the pleasure of that kiss? From the standpoint of the *Âtmā* there is no other but Itself. 793. A body embraces another body. It is Vāyu who presides over the sense of touch of both. Now who is to get pleasure from that pleasure? For the *Ātmā* is no other but Itself. 794. Thus it is evident that the multitude of divinities are not the cause of joy and sorrow. All these divinities cease to exist in relation to the *Âtmā*, through the fact of there being no such thing as differences belonging to It.

795. If, therefore, it is asserted that if the gods cause pain to the body, the one conscious of possessing that body will feel pain, he, who thinks this, is a big fool. This cannot be true. 796. Consider a single body as a city, and one is a citizen of that city. Now in that body (which is the city) it is assumed there is but one man. Now who is going to worry over another's sorrow? 797. Or supposing in the wildness of frenzy one strikes oneself with one's own hand. Here the only sharer of one's pain, and the only object for anger, is oneself. 798. When one sees that one is but the One, how can there be any thought of pain from another? Who is to be angry with whom? One is but the One with-

out another. 799. So if I think of myself thus, "I am the universal *Ātmā.* I am the divinities. I am mankind," then thus thinking who is there to give pain to whom? Who is there for me to get angry with? 800. As one thus thinks within himself, it is evident that joys and sorrows can absolutely never come from divinities. There is no such thing as divinity-caused sorrow.

THE ĀTMĀ IS NOT THE CAUSE OF SORROW.

801. That the *Ātmā* is the cause of joy and sorrow is to me altogether without proof. With the *Ātmā* there is no such thing as cause and effect, joy or sorrow. 802. The *Âtmā* is absolutely alone and One. How can there be with Him either joy or sorrow? Those, therefore, who say the *Âtmā* is the giver of joy and sorrow are irrational fools. 803. Just as when *ghi* is melted, it has no form nor color. But when it is congealed it looks white in color, and is in the form of granules. 804. Now when the granules of the *ghi* assume that form, no joy or pain is given by one to the other. So the *Ātmā,* which is alone and One, is many only in form. 805. In water there are waves of water. When these waves come in contact with one another they give no joy or pain to one another. So is it with the Supreme *Ātmā* as related to animate and inanimate things. 806. The Supreme *Âtmā* is alone and One. It is many only in the form of Its Oneness. There is nothing separate from it. So to whom can there belong joy or sorrow? 807. The *Ātmā* in its totality is in the form of joy. The appearance of variety is a Mayā product, imaginary, and false like a dream. 808. Looking at a mirage, it looks like water; but it is absolutely dry. So that which appears as the vast expanse of matter is false

and Māyā-begotten. 809. Where false and Māyā-produced Duality appears, there exists the *Ātmā* alone and One. Recognizing this, joy and sorrow immediately disappear, and there is no place for anger. 810. Where one recognizes one's oneness as *Ātmā*, there can be no joy or sorrow, for who is to be angry with whom? There is but One alone. 811. Where there is the consciousness of being *Ātmā,* there will be the non-existence of Duality. Joy and sorrow must then be meaningless, and there can be no place for anger. 812. Those who do not recognize the fact that they are *Ātmā,* and who regard joy and sorrow as real, even though they may be persons versed in the *Vedas* and *Shāstras,* are conquered by anger. 813. But he who recognizes in all creatures his oneness with them as *Ātmā*, who is there then to give any pain to whom? Who can get angry with whom? There exists but one *Ātmā* in all. 814. That the *Ātmā* is the giver of joy or sorrow is therefore not a fact. Even fools do not give themselves pain.

THE PLANETS ARE NOT THE CAUSE OF SORROW.

815. There is a fourth theory that it is the planets that are the givers of sorrow. But this cannot be. Listen attentively, while I explain why. 816. The body that is born from the mother's (*janani*) womb is called *jana* [man]. The contact of the planet with a person at the time of his birth, continues from the time of his birth during the course of the planet. 817. The auspicious and inauspicious planets under which one is born, occupying the twelfth or eighth place in the zodiac, are the cause of joy or sorrow,

but the *Âtmā* is untouched, being unrelated to the course of the planets. 818. There is no such thing as birth to the *Ātmā*, then how can the planets influence it? Where the field has not been sown, what have the mice to nibble at? 819. If you have not even built a house, how can its upper storey burn? As there is no such thing as birth to the *Âtmā*, how can the course of the planets affect It? 820. The course of the planets affect the body. But the *Ātmā* is unrelated to any experience of a body. Just as a crow cannot fly upwards to Kailās, so the planets cannot reach the *Âtmā*. 821. Just as a fly does not attempt to taste fire; just as the kite does not swoop down on the moon, so the planets have no power to exert an influence over the *Ātmā*. 822. The *Ātmā* is the all of every thing. So it is the all of the planets. If they gave pain to the *Âtmā*, it would be giving pain to themselves. 823. The body is inanimate without understanding and ignorant. It does not understand the philosophy of joy and sorrow. In thinking that they are giving joy or sorrow to the *Ātmā*, the planets would be giving pain to themselves. 824. One can never cause pain to oneself. So the planets, in their courses, can never give pain to the *Âtmā*.

825. There is a state of enmity between the planets. Planets give trouble to planets. Listen to the explanation of how this occurs. 826. On the authority of Astronomy, Saturn and Mars are enemies of the Sun. Jupiter and Venus are hostile to one another. Jupiter is a bitter enemy of the Moon. 827. Some of these planets are swift in their motion. Other planets move slowly. Some are very swift, some are very crooked in their orbits. These come together with all their differences. 828. These enemies

come together in one constellation. During one step of the way they live together. But Rāhu swallows the Sun, and the Sun puts the Moon into conjunction. 829. Thus planets are related to planets. They give one another trouble. But I, the *Âtmā,* am unrelated to them. How can they give me joy or sorrow? 830. You smash some jewelry to pieces, but the gold is not broken up. So although the planets give pain to one another, what joy or sorrow can there be to me, the *Ātmā*? 831. In the arena there is fighting and pulling of hair, but the ground does not suffer blows. So I, *Âtmā,* am untouched by the evil influences of the planets. 832. A menstruating woman walking on the ground does not defile the ground. So while planet troubles planet, I am untouched by joy and sorrow. 833. So whatever joy or sorrow arises from the planets in connection with my body, it does not touch Me, who am *Ātmā.* So who is to be angry with whom? 834. He in whom no joy or sorrow arises, can feel no anger. So for this reason there can be no joy or sorrow from the planets.

ONE'S KARMA IS NOT THE CAUSE OF SORROW.

835. Some say that it is one's *Karma,* through which comes illusion to men. But the *Ātmā,* being without *Karma,* how can it be pained through *Karma,* which is inanimate? 836. *Karma,* through its inanimateness is strictly limited. The *Ātmā,* in its form of Intelligence, is absolutely pure. It can never, therefore, be related to a *Karma*-produced pain. 837. If one can confine the sun in darkness; if one can confine a forest fire in straw; if a tick can put its mouth to a flame; 838. if chaff can constrain a tornado;

if the mud of a puddle can hold the Moon, then only can the *Ātmā,* voluntarily bound, suffer *karma*-begotten joys or sorrows. 839. That the *Ātmā* destroys *karma* and *akarma,* makes a bonfire of joy and sorrow, or is a partaker of the fruits of *Karma,* is the idea of foolish simpletons. 840. Do one's dream-children come to visit one in one's awakened state? No more can the joys and sorrows from *Karma* afflict the *Ātmā.* 841. Just as an ant cannot walk over fire, so the *Ātmā* cannot be soiled by the filth of *karma.* One cannot slit the ether with a weapon. So the *Ātmā* cannot be touched by the effects of *Karma.*

842. All that comes from *Karma* is begotten of Ignorance. The *Ātmā* is pure and beyond all, both Knowledge and Ignorance. Those who think that It feels the *karma*-begotten joys and sorrows, are fools, resulting from their illusions through consciousness of body. 843. *Karma* is absolutely inanimate. The *Ātmā* is absolutely pure. *Karma* appears in variety. The *Ātmā* is the infinite all. *Karma* is ever bound and strictly limited. The *Ātmā* exists in the form of Intelligence and Joy. 844. *Karma* is illusory, begotten of *Māyā.* The *Ātmā* is ever unassociated with *Māyā.* *Karma* has no acquaintance with Brahma. Where Brahma is there is no *Karma.* 845. There is no serpenthood in the rope, mistaken for a serpent. Can it then bite and spread its poison? So in the true nature of the *Ātmā,* any relation with *Karma* is a false assumption. Can it then harm the *Ātmā?* 846. The idea of *Karma*-begotten joys and sorrows prevail among the strict Believers in *Karma,* but this is like saying, "The beloved grandson of a barren queen is ruling the world in his royal power." 847. Thus *Karma* itself being illusory, how can it give joy and sorrow? And knowing this for a certainty, who is to

be angry with whom? 848. Thus it cannot be that *Karma* is the giver of joy and sorrow.

*KĀLA IS NOT THE CAUSE OF SORROW.

But you may say, "It is *Kāla* that gives joy and sorrow." But this also cannot happen. 849. Kāla, in the cold season causes distress through cold. In the Hot season he lets loose blasts of heat. In the Rainy season he sends rain, and brings to the ground even three storey lime-built dwellings. 850. Pouring down rain in torrents, in ceaseless showers, he does not let one open one's eyes. He distresses living things, and causes stringency of food. 851. By the lack of food beasts, birds and other animals are distressed. At that time no one feels joy or sorrow, for the giver of the sorrow is one's own Kāla. 852. Kāla devours the world by his intense heat, his intense cold, his letting loose of mighty winds, and the world trembles at Kāla. 853. Even the gods, when they hear about Kāla, violently tremble. Then what must happen to others? Even Brahmadeva's heart beats with fright. 854. Through excessive rain, and through the absence of rain, Kāla brings distress to men. At the end of time he brings suddenly the final universal destruction. The giver of pain to the world is this mighty Kāla.

855. The above is what some wise people say, but in their wisdom they have become fools. For notice! Kāla is God Himself, the giver of happiness to all,

---

*Kāla, the divinity presiding over time, death, final destruction, and the forces of Nature.

KĀLA IS GOD AND BENEVOLENT

856. He who says that Kāla is different from God is unintelligent, dull of understanding and ignorant. Kāla is God Himself, wholly merciful, the *Ātmā* of the Universe. 857. Kāla, raining down water at the proper season rejoices mankind, oppressed by the heat. Cooling the earth, he causes the fields to be newly sown. 858. If at that time the cold did not come, the sown seed would turn to ashes. So raining down cold he makes the fields fertile. 859. At the time of the harvest the humidity is of no value to the fields or to men, so Kāla, in the hot season dries up the moisture. 860. Thus by cold, heat, and rain, Kāla works for the good of creatures. He who finds this difficult to understand does so because he is confused by the illusion from consciousness of body. 861. Taking away one's utterly worn out garments, and clothing one in new raiment with great care, such is the act of the benevolent Kāla, and yet the mad call him an enemy. 862. Kāla, at the proper time destroys the weak and age enfeebled body, and gives it a new body. Such is the benevolence of Kāla to mankind. 863. He takes away the old and gives the new in its place. Only mad men will call such a benevolent Kāla a malevolent being, for they are greedy for their bodily passions. 864. Mankind, according to their desires, and according to their earnest longings, find Kāla merciful, and He gives them the body they desire. 865. As at the time of some great festival the father, throwing away the worn out garments, gives his son new garments, so Kāla, at the final destruction (gives a new creation). 866. At the final destruction Kāla destroys the old body and gives new and glorious ones to all in His great mercy. 867. Thus Kāla is merciful. He who calls Him an enemy is a babbler.

The *Ātmā* of the world is Kāla. He gives the irritation of pain to no one. 868. The strong desires of men center in their bodies, and Kāla, according to their desires gives them bodies one after the other. And so comes the succession of births and deaths. 869. He who truly wishes for a state of unconsciousness-of-body, Kāla destroys the consciousness of self being the body, and gives him the calmness of His own joy, removing the succession of births and deaths. 870. According to one's desires Kāla gives them the fulfilment of them. Those who are blind, through the seductions of the body, do not understand that Kāla is absolutely merciful. 871. He, whose knowledge comprehends that Kāla is the *Ātmā* of each individual, from whom can he think to receive pain? For there is no other than himself. 872. That I am a giver of pain, and over there is one who suffers the pain, such an idea of Duality is impossible. The sole *Ātmā* of the world is *Kāla*. 873. The two, *Ātmā* and *Kāla,* are one. Now who gets pleasure from whom? There cannot be such a thing as their giving pain to one another. 874. Mirage-water is a name only. There is not even a drop of water there. So to suppose a world-expanse to the *Ātmā* is a mere illusion of the *mana.* 875. The *Ātmā,* in Its oneness is without differentiation. It is He who is generally called Kāla. A living being is a portion of the pure Intelligence. It cannot be evilly affected by supposing a separateness from *Kāla* and the like. 876. Can fire burn fire? Can the sun be scorched by heat? Can the ocean be sunk by the might of its waves? Can lamp-black make the darkness black? 877. Can the Himālaya mountains be made to tremble by a snow flake? Can *ghi* make *ghi* undigestible? So the *Ātmā* can endure a limitless amount of Duality in the activities of the power of *Kāla.*

878. No one is willing to harm himself by way of self-enmity. So *Kāla,* can never evilly affect the *Ātmā* by the infliction of Duality. 879. So where there is this oneness of the *Ātmā,* without differentiation, there the evil effect of *Kāla* is impossible. Where there is no differentiation there can be no evil effects from Duality, for here who is to be angry with whom? 880. I am *Jiva,* I am *Shiva.* I am *Ātmā,* I am Kāla. So all this confusion of pain from Duality is false. On whom am I to dash my waves of wrath? 881. That *Kāla,* then, is the giver of pain, cannot be, if one thinks aright. The *Ātmā* cannot feel the evil effects of either joy or sorrow.

882. The above mentioned six causes of joy and sorrow cannot evilly affect the *Ātmā,* when one properly reasons, according to the Scripture, "*Nāyam jano etc*". 883. Aside from the above six, from the point of view of causing evil to the *Ātmā,* one cannot find any other cause anywhere, composed of the three *guṇas.* 884. Nothing can cause an evil effect on the *Ātmā.* That which evilly affects men is a consciousness-of-body. The explanation of this the Mendicant gives as follows.

THE EFFECT OF CONSCIOUSNESS-OF-BODY.

885. The *Ātmā* is qualitiless and pure, anterior to every thing, Joy itself, absolutely complete in Itself, *sat-chidānanda,* [existent-intelligence-joy]. The evil effect of Duality cannot enter into It. 886. How, by what, by whom can there be the evil effects from Duality in the sphere of the *Ātmā*? There can be no evil effect through cause, action and effect. 887. Where there is no internal difference there can be no evil effects from Duality, to that

which is Itself joy. Nor can there be any connection of pain with that which is perfect. The *Ātmā* is supreme joy Itself and exists alone.

888. Question: If there cannot be any relation between the *Ātmā* and Duality, and if the body, through its inanimateness is unconscious of Duality, who is it that feels the great evils from the effects of Duality?

889. Answer. The chief cause for the experiencing of joy and sorrow, through the experience of births and deaths, is consciousness-of-body. The explanation of this is also beyond one's reasoning power. 890. Just as a woman, staying with her husband, may commit adultery, and become pregnant through another man, and yet no one may know the fact. 891. Such is the marvel of Consciousness-of-body. By connection with the *Ātmā,* as Intelligence, it causes the illusory idea of being a living being, experiencing joy and sorrow by its own will. 892. Just as a deceitful minister of the king commits wrong, using the power of the king, and brings trouble in many ways to the king's subjects. So is the Consciousness-of-body in the body. 893. Or as when the iron by fire becomes one with fire, who then can take hold of it with his hand? It would burn every one who did so. 894. So the consciousness of Intelligence, arousing the idea of body, and thereby producing joy and sorrow, births and deaths, who is there to prevent this? 895. The body in a dream is only *mana*-stuff, but that body has a *mana.* So this body of mine is but of *mana* itself, and through its consciousness-of-body has made it a solid substance. 896. In the form of the idea of cause and effect, worldly-existence exists through the consciousness of *mana,* which increasing joy

and painful sorrow, itself experiences birth and death. 897. In passing through all one's experiences, one suffers many evils, and still one does not discard self-consciousness, and on the contrary emphasizes the idea of *Ātmā* and body. 898. And even at the Final Destruction the consciousness-of-body is not discarded. Even in that Destruction the consciousness does not melt away, and one continues to experience joy and sorrow. 899. One's life is as when one looks at the *jāsvandi* flower through a crystal. The crystal gets the color of the flower, although that is not its real color. 900. There is no joy or sorrow to the *Ātmā,* but it appears as if it were possessed with a body. This pleasurable misconception is because of the imagination. 901. "This body is mine" So saying to oneself, one accepts it through consciousness and thereby becomes involved in the whirlpool of births and deaths, and becomes an experiencer of joy and sorrow. 902. In accordance with this reasoning, the wise man, who has gained his knowledge from his *guru,* although carrying on his life among men, or in forests, does not have the consciousness-of-body. 903. It is true that such enlightened men, who know themselves as *Ātmā,* may, by the action of deeds in a former birth, suffer many kinds of joys and sorrows among creatures, yet the idea of being Âtmā is not shaken. 904. Hence they have no anger arising against any one. No wrath comes into their minds. "I alone exist in all the Three-worlds." By means of this thought they are entirely without the idea of Duality. 905. Such an one looks at the ups and downs of life without fear in his mind. He calls no one a stranger, but calls all his own relatives, they being his own *Âtmā.* 906. He does not have the idea of equality, inequality or difference, for the knower is in his very nature without differentiation.

He has no fear or pain from any one, and is always happy and joyous. 907. The chief characteristic of a Saint therefore, is that while enduring insults, persecution and a succession of indignities, he is full of joy. That characteristic is the Seeker's means (for the highest spiritual attainment).

RIGHT-THINKING COMES FROM TRUST IN GOD.

908. "By an unusual good fortune taking place in my former birth I see arisen in me the conviction that I am *Atmā,* without a second. By means of this conviction I endure the various sorrows of life, recognizing no duality. 909. The natural characteristic of a Saint is his endurance of the joys and sorows that come from duality. And this is my chief means [*sădhana*]. Through this I conquer my *mana.* 910. This is the supreme means for acquiring the Supreme-Spiritual-Riches. This indeed was the conviction of the great rishis. This is the worship one renders to Vaikuṇṭha [Vishṇu]. By this is acquired the conviction that one is *Atmā* alone. 911. By means of this the sorrows from duality do not afflict one. By means of this one obtains eternal happiness. It is Right-Thinking [*viveka*] that saves us in the difficult passage through *samsāra.* 912. In order to go across the difficult sea of *samsāra* in this life, this Right-Thinking [*viveka*] is a well devised ship. Here the *sadguru* is the helmsman, and takes us across to the Beyond. 913. How to get possession of this Right-Thinking [*viveka*] one need not worry over. With trust and sincerity one must approach God. 914. Putting away shame, due to popular reputation, casting down the load of pride, one must approach God. Then one will

receive this Right-Thinking [*viveka*]. 915. Just as an infant, with complete trust, comes for help in everything to its mother, so with the same exclusive trust one should constantly approach Hari. 916. If one approaches Hari for help, birth and death will not so much as show their faces to him. What Duality is there that can harm one, if Hari is there to protect His *Bhakta*.

HOW ONE IS TO APPROACH GOD.

917. The giver of full Deliverance is Mukunda [Krishṇa]. But how is one to approach Him? In His infinity he is qualitiless. Who can approach Him there. 918. So be it, but though absolutely qualitiless (*nirguṇ*) in His form of Hari, if in contemplating His qualitiful (*saguṇ*) image, that possesses form, one firmly holds this form in one's mind, all sorrows from duality are destroyed. 919. If the image of Hari does not come into one's mind completely, then one should at least hold fast to His feet. In doing so births and deaths will flee away. In their fear of themselves all Dualities will flee away. 920. If one is unable to hold fast to His feet, then one should repeat His names, for merely at His name Yama and Kāla tremble. 921. Where there is the constant repetition aloud of the names of Hari, there death comes to Death itself. Births get a black face, and becoming ashamed flee away. 922. Before the shouting of Rām's name, what are the poor, wretched sorrows from Duality! All fears of this worldly existence fly away while His name is being sung aloud. 923. In the voice of one uninterruptedly and loudly uttering His name, Chakrapāṇi [Krishṇa] is Himself the utterance. There *Riddhi* and *Siddhi* carry water for him. *Mukti* is his slave. 924. If with trust and undoubting mind the

bhakta reverences the *Saguṇ* or the *Nirguṇ,* or repeats His names, there takes place, as a result, goodness of heart. 925. When in one's trustful feelings there is the love of God, that alone should be considered as true *bhakti.* Shripati [Krishṇa] is pleased with this feeling of love, and gives His peace to the Seeker. 926. Included in this peace is the disappearance of the millions of joys and sorrows and the Universe becomes filled to overflowing with supreme joy. And then no where does one see the Duality of I and Thou. 927. With this conception of there being no differentiation, if one serves the glorious feet of Mukunda, [Krishṇa] I, Mukunda myself, will certainly save him. 928. The instant I say "I will save" that instant he is saved. Less than it takes time to say it, he who becomes the beloved child of Hari, has thereafter no *samsāra.*"

KRISHṆA'S PRAISE OF THE REPENTANT MISER.

929. Thus did the Mendicant sing his song. It immensely pleased Śri Krishṇa, and overflowing with joy he patted the head of Uddhava. 930. "I wish my Uddhava should also possess this my peace," and with this compassionate feeling Shripati talked to Uddhava. 931. He, from whose breath the *Vedas* were born, from whose feet the famous Ganges flows, He, whose name cuts in two the bonds of this worldly-existence, He, Govinda, with his own lips talked to Uddhava. 932. For this reason the good fortune of Uddhava was great, who having pleased Sharaṅgadhara [Krishṇa] was shown the home of His peace, where it abides for ever.

933. "Uddhava, listen attentively. Having spoiled the wealth of the miser, I have become pleased with the miser. I have made him the possessor of Right-Thinking [*viveka*] and changed him to a *Vairāgi.* 934. He who was a miser, who would not even eat sufficiently, whose name people would not mention, has become well known, through his distaste for worldly things. His story is ever on my lips. 935. His name is on my lips. I myself am glorifying his deeds for a man of Right-Thinking [*viveka*] and *Vairāgya* is very dear to me. 936. There is nothing superior to *Vairāgya* in the world. He who in truth possesses the True-Right-Thinking [*viveka*] and *vairāgya,* is my inner soul itself, O Uddhava. 937. He, who is possessed of Right-Thinking and *Vairāgya,* is in me. I am in his words. He is wholly sold to me.

938. The avaricious man lost every bit of his property, and with the property went his pride of reputation, and with his pride went the joys and painful sorrows from Duality. 939. As his wealth left him he became one indifferent to worldly things, and he became a strict *sannyāsi.* As he wandered over the country, begging his food, he was insulted by evil men with harsh language. 940. But though persecuted with many forms of maltreatment, yet he never wavered. He courageously performed his special duties without the thought of duality. 941. He had the special characteristics of a *sannyāsi* in the thought "I am outside of body. I am Nārāyaṇa Himself. I have lost truly all consciousness-of-body." Having thus thought, he no longer wavered. 942. As when one's shadow is smitten, one has no fear or doubts, so when those evil men smote his body, this mendicant, without bodily consciousness, had neither

sorrow nor fear. 943. Although his body had much suffering, yet he sang the song of his being outside the body, and this I have already described."

KRISHṆA TELLS THE CAUSE OF JOY AND SORROW.

944. The true cause of joy and sorrow, namely, because of misconception, is described by Śri Krishna Himself.

945. "One's Ignorance, which comes from not knowing, is the reason why the *mana* produces the idea of *mana,* and the *mana* differentiating every thing causes one the experiences of joy and sorrow. 946. The *Ātmā* is void of differences, but the *mana,* imagining enemy, friend, or one indifferent, disturbs the whole of itself. 947. The *mana,* thus forcing the idea of difference, is the ignorance of the man, and by it comes the sorrow from duality, and the hardship of *samsāra* to the deluded person. 948. The *mana* is the cause of joy and sorrow. *Samsāra* [this worldly-existence] is *mana*-imagined." How to control that *mana* Śri Krishṇa Himself relates.

THE CONFLICT BETWEEN VIVEKA AND MANA.

949. "He who intends to end the sorrows of *samsāra* must of necessity hold his *mana* in control. There is no other that gives one sorrow in all the three-worlds but the *mana.* 950. The *mana* is intensely fickle. It cannot easily be made steady. One must, therefore, let Right-Thinking [*viveka*] have free scope, which never recognizes any differences. 951. That the *mana* may not slip away from Right-Thinking[*viveka*] one should handcuff them together.

952. So that when false thought comes to the *mana*, Right-Thinking may give it strong blows. Where wrong thought creates wrong doing there Right-Thinking [*viveka*] may rush in to drive it away. 953. The *mana* goes towards evil desire and anger. Right-Thinking [*viveka*] grasping it by the hair, draws it back. When the *mana* goes to indulge in insults, Right-Thinking gives it a fisticuff. 954. The *mana* says, "I want freedom for my sensual desires." Right-Thinking replies, "Here is the club of Indifference-to-worldly-desires [*vairāgya*]." The *mana* runs after its imaginations. Right-Thinking at once seizes it by the hair. 955. The *mana* with lust runs after another's wife or wealth. Right-Thinking [*viveka*] arrives on the scene and begins a struggle. 956. This struggle between the *mana* and Right-Thinking[*viveka*] comes as a complaint before the *sadguru*. In order to judge between the two he shuts them up in the prison of non-duality. 957. At the sight of that place the characteristic of the *mana* is changed, and dropping the consciousness-of-body is reconciled with Right-Thinking. 958. Thus the *mana*-characteristics of the *mana* disappear, and *viveka* forgets its characteristic of restraining. The idea, which the individual being has, of being an individual melts away, and all is One, the one Substance, without a second. 959. Just as a golden ornament in the form of a snake, exhibits hood and tail according to its serpent form, but, even without breaking up the ornament in the form of a cobra, the gold, from the point of view of the gold, forgets its cobra shape. 960 So knowing that one is the Universal Substance, without breaking up its form of the Universe, the living being forgets that it is living, and the *mana* loses the idea of *mana*. 961. Thus joined to *Viveka* [Right-Thinking] my *mana* enters

my true form, where the *mana* does not have its characteristic of *mana,* and this is called the control of the *mana.*"

PEACE THROUGH THE CONTROL OF THE MANA.

962. "Listen, O Uddhava, you, Wish-jewel-of-wise-minds, you Chief jewel-of-Lord-*Viveka,* Chief of the *bhaktas*! Make use of this control of the *mana.*" 963. Lord Krishṇa was overcome by his affection, and said to Uddhava, "Tāta! Be one who reverently makes an effort for the control of the *mana.* 964. He who with determination controls his *mana,* and puts away the *mana*-begotten differences, Peace will not know how to leave him, just as a mother does not know how to forsake her infant. 965. If pure Peace has entered one, no Duality, of any kind, can harm him. And this is the well known Yoga, which the great Yogis have described. 966. As one loses the idea of *samsār,* and as one's functioning is in one's intelligence-state, *Jiva* and *Shiva* [the individual and the universal soul] become one, and this state of being is called *Yogasañgraha.* 967. When such peace from *Yogasañgraha* exists, the Seeker is not harmed by the Dualities.

THE VALUE OF THE BHIKSHUGITA EXTOLLED.

Moreover he who possesses a reverential devotion to this Bhikshugita, thereby gains release from the Dualities. 968. In order to obtain peace the millions of methods will not avail. But if one holds this Song of the Mendicant [Bhikshugita] in one's heart, peace comes easily to him as a Seeker of it. 969. Adherence to the Yoga, Knowledge of Brahma, all is included in this Song-of-the-Mendicant. He who attentively holds it in his heart, Peace becomes his slave. 970. He who in the quietness of his mind keeps in his heart the true meaning of the Song-of-the-Mendicant, the blows of Duality will not harm him, for through his enlightenment he will possess the greatest peace. 971. It is not a strange thing to say that understanding the *Bhikshugita* brings peace. He, who, with reverence listens to it, will not be harmed by the Dualities. 972. As when a husband,long absent in a foreign land, sends a letter, and the wife listens with reverence while it is being read, so one should listen to the Song-of-the-Mendicant with the greatest concentration of mind. 973. If a son has strayed from his home, and the mother gets trace of him, and hears rumours of his whereabouts, how excited she becomes. 974. The relatives, living near the mother, have sympathy with her because of friendship, but none have the same violent emotions in their hearts as does the mother. 975. So he whose heart melts at the listening to the Song-of-the-Mendicant, and who overflows with goodness of heart, he cannot be overcome by the Dualities.

976. But even supposing there may not be the reverent listening to the Song-of-the-Mendicant, still if there is the constant reading of it, through its power the Dualities will not touch such an one. 977. The moment a mad elephant smells a lion he wildly flees away. So from the reading of the Song-of-the-Mendicant there comes the smashing to pieces of the Dualities. 978. He who with an unavaricious mind sits down with saints and other good

people, and explains the Song-of-the-Mendicant, such an one is untouched by the Dualities. 979. By reading or listening to the Song-of-the-Mendicant, the Dualities are kept away." This inner mystic power of the song, Shri Krishṇa understood, and he told it to Uddhava for his good.

THE SONG-OF-THE-MENDICANT FOR THE SALVATION OF THE WORLD.

980. The fruits from listening to the Song-of-the-Mendicant, Shripati's [Krishṇa] lips have related. How can I sufficiently describe the good fortune of the mendicant. Blessed is he, the one most blest in the Three-worlds. 981. He who in the union of *Viveka* and *Vairāgya* is able to endure the excessive sufferings from Dualities, he is most beloved by Krishṇa, as he explained to Uddhava. 982. This is the benevolent deed rendered to the world by Uddhava, that Krishṇa should open to him the treasures of the mystic knowledge of the Beyond, by revealing the meaning of the Song-of-the-Mendicant. 983. If Uddhava had not asked about peace, why would Shripati have told him about it? It was because Krishṇa loved Uddhava, that He exhorted him in various ways. 984. This means salvation for the dull minded. By this means the humble are saved. For the salvation of the world Śri Krishṇa, the Life-of-the-world, told these things, using Uddhava as his opportunity. 985. Śri Krishṇa related this Song of the Mendicant, [Bhikshugita] the cream of the *Vedas* and other *Shāstras*, the substance of the *Upanishads*, and the mystic meaning of spoken words. 986. By it Śri Krishṇa, through the

favor of a *bhakta,* made known the most recondite knowledge of how one's *ātmā* is related to oneself. 987. By it the *Jiva*-characteristic of the *Jiva* [individual soul] disappears. The *Shiva*-characteristic of the *Shiva* [universal soul] sinks out of existence. The harmfulness of Duality is broken, and the treasure house of happiness is opened.

EKNĀTH CHARACTERIZES HIS MARATHI VERSION OF THE BHIKSHUGITA.

988. Where the *Vedas* have had to be silent, where the wordy *shāstras* have had to be ashamed, there this most recondite Song-of-the-Mendicant, I, Eknath, have rendered into the Prākṛit [Marathi]. 989. As Śri Rām made the stone slab to float, that was sinking in the water, so through the favor of Janārdan, I, dull, foolish and ignorant, have been chosen to make known this knowledge. 990. Ahilyā, the adulteress, the moment she (as a stone slab) was touched by Shri Rām's foot, became a name, the morning repetition of which causes the washing away of sin. 991. So, by the doings of the favor of my *sadguru,* he has made me so to speak, that my dull, foolish voice is honoured among the saints and wise men. 992. He, whom Sarasvati [goddess of speech] makes to speak, he, though a mute, can repeat the *Vedas.* So, Janārdan has done for me, in making me repeat this Song-of-the-Mendicant in the Prākṛit [Marāthi]. 993. He, in whose hands are the marks of royalty, all pay him respect. So, Janārdan has indeed made my voice a leading one. 994. A mother is very happy when she hears the prattle of her child. So my uncouth voice has been made lovable among saints and good men.

EKNĀTH GIVES THE GLORY TO HIS GURU, JANĀRDAN.

995. And who should take it upon his head to say "I, my superior language, my inferior language, etc." Janārdan has taken away this egoism, and it is he who causes me to relate this story. 996. To begin with, this is the Śri Bhāgavata Purāṇa. In it is the eleventh *skandha,* with its deep meaning. And in that *skandha* is the Bhikshugita with its extremely recondite meaning, teaching non-duality. 997. I, Eknāth, am not the only author of this Commentary on the Bhikshugita. Janārdan has taken away that idea of sole authorship, and it is he who has caused me to compose this writing, explaining the book. 998. Janārdan has made its authorship not by one or by many. He has caused to be related the marvel of the equality of the apparently dual.

999. Ekā [Eknāth] comes as a suppliant to Janārdan. He has become one with Janārdan. And through this oneness (of himself and myself) this Song-of-the-Mendicant has been completed. 1000. The *Guru* of my *Guru,* the great Guru Dattātreya, the chief Yogi of Yogis, has been pleased because of this Bhikshugita. 1001. Assuring me of his great pleasure, he placed his hands upon me in blessing, and wagged his head in delight, because of the supreme value of this book.*

---

*See the story of Dattātreya's revelation of Himself to Eknāth when a young disciple of Janārdan, in the volume on "Eknāth," in Poet-Saints of Mahārāshṭra Series, page 18, 166—208, No. 2.

1002. Ekā [Eknāth] comes as a suppliant to Janārdan. Let the listener be attentive, for in the next chapter Śri Krishṇa will explain the subject of *Prakṛiti* and *Purush.* 1003. If any one takes thoughtfully to his heart this story of *Prakṛiti* and *Purush,* he will be able to say "I am beyond all dualities of joy and sorrow, through the self enlightened *Ātmā.*

1004. My *sāshtāṅg namaskār* to all saints and good men. My prostrate obeisance to my listeners. Ekā Janārdan calls attention to the very delightful discourse which is to follow.

In the Great Purāṇa, the Śri Bhāgavata, in the eleventh *skandha,* in the discussion between Śri Krishna and Uddhava, in the Commentary by Ekā [Eknāth] is the development of the story called the Bhikshugita, the twenty-third chapter. Obeisance to Śri Krishṇa. The 23rd chapter, 62 Sanskrit *ślokas,* 1004 Marathi verses.

APPENDIX I

GLOSSARY OF MARATHI WORDS USED IN THE TRANSLATIONS AND OF WORDS WHOSE TRANSLATION PRESENTS DIFFICULTIES.

It might have been possible to have used fewer Marāthi words in these translations, but where there is no English word that exactly expresses the Marāthi word, or where it requires a whole English phrase to express the meaning of a simple Marāthi word, it has seemed to me better to keep the Marāthi word, so familiar to India, and let the English reader learn its meaning by its context, or by the following glossary. English literature is already enriched by many Marāthi words. I see no reason why it should not still further enrich itself.

There are certain words, that are untranslatable except by a long explanation; others, where even the English word conveys only a part of the Marāthi meaning. I have translated these words and expressions as best I could, but it seems worth while to include some of these words in a glossary in order that the reader, familiar with both languages, may understand why I have used and the special English word or words, sometimes in opposition to Dictionary authorities, even Molesworth. Usage has to be considered, as well as etymological meaning. The glossary will furnish the examples that have suggested the above remarks. I have used Molesworth's definitions freely, as carrying authority.

RULES FOR PRONUNCIATION.

a as u in utter, butter, hut.
ā as a in father, far.
i as i in in
ī as ee in thee.
u as ou in you
ū as oo in food
e as a in ape, age.
ai as i in island, decline.
o as o in open, over.
au as ou in proud, plough.
g always hard, as g in gate, get.
ch as ch in church.
sh or as sh in shine.

Other letters are pronounced very nearly as in English words.

A

Abhaṅg. A particular metrical composition in praise of the Deity. It is the popular meter of the poet-saints in their hymns of praise; the *abhaṅgs* of Eknāth, the *abhaṅgs* of Tukārām etc.

Abheda-bhakta. A *bhakta* who has the conception of no-difference (*abheda*) between the *paramātmā* [Supreme-*Ātmā*] and the individual *ātmā*. *Abheda-bhakti* is the worship of God in harmony with the conception of the identity of the *paramātmā* and the soul [*ātmā*] of the worshipper.

Adhelā. A copper coin worth half a pice.

Agnihotri. The priest who maintains the Sacrificial fire.

Amrita. Nectar. The drink that prevents death.

Anugraha. Favor, grace, kindness, Instructing in mystical verses or incantations.

Anushṭhāna. Performance of certain ceremonies and works in propitiation of a god.

Avatār. Etymologically it means "one who has descended." A divine *avatār* is the coming down to earth of such a divine being, as for example, Vishṇu in the form of Krishṇa, or Rāma. In Indian mythology, as well as in all popular conceptions, these *avatārs* are for the sake of combating some evil condition or conditions in this world, or, to save the world from its sin and misery.

Human *avatārs* are also recognized (*mānava avatār*), that is, a good man who has died, reappears later in some other good man, to carry on, or to complete, the work of the former. Eknāth is spoken of as an *avatār* of Dnyānadeva, and Tukārām as an *avatār* of Nāmadeva. Or Eknāth, for example, is spoken of as an *avatār* of God, making him, therefore, both divine and human.

Achārya. Head of a religious order or sect.

Ārati. 1. The ceremony of (waving around an idol, guru etc.,) a platter containing a burning lamp. 2 The platter and lamp waved. 3 The piece of poetry chanted on the occasion of the ceremony of waving, expressing praise or worship.

Áshrama. 1. The abode of saints and rishis. 2. The word is also applied to four conditions of living, the *Brahmacharya,* or the period of chaste youth, and study; The *grihastha,* the householder in his married and secular life; The *vānaprastha,* who as age comes on passes his worldly cares over to others, and goes into the forest for meditation, and the fourth the *Sannyāsi,* who entirely abandons all worldly cares, delights and passions, and is wholly absorbed in contemplation or the worship of God. These four *āshramas* are considered the ideal life for a Brāhman.

'Átmā. The soul, the soul of the universe, the human soul, the vivifying principle, the self, the ego. For clearness the soul of the universe is spoken of as *parama* [supreme] *ātmā,* to distinguish it from the individual *ātmā,* the two, however, in Vedāntic philosophy being identical. Brahma, or the *Parama-ātmā,* partially defined as *satchidānanda* [Existent, intelligence, joy] is the sole existing substance. The universe, as it appears in animate and inanimate forms, with their special names, is but the form in which the *ātmā,* the *paramātmā,* or *Brahma* manifests itself. The human soul, or *ātmā,* is, therefore, only a form in which the *paramātmā* appears. The "great sentence" *ahambramhāsmi,* "I am Brahma," is the conscious acceptance of the philosophic postulate of the oneness of the soul of the universe with the individual soul.

B

Bachnāg. Poisonous root of the Gloriosa Superba.

Bhajan. 1. Adoration or worship. 2 Repeating the names of God as an act of worship. 3 A hymn, or verses sung in the worship of God.

Bhakta. 1. A worshipper, votary, or follower of; one devoted or attached to. While the above definition is etymologically correct, in usage, by the poet-saints, there is connected with it a moral idea. A *bhakta* implies a really pious man. A hypocrite is not a *bhakta,* though technically and outwardly he might appear to be one. 2. A special religious class devoted to the religious life.

As the different manifestations of God, and the various *avatārs* appeal differently to different minds, there is a personal choice as well as the traditional, or family choice of the special manifestation of God. There is therefore, a *Vishnubhakta,* a *Śivabhakta,* a *Haribhakta,* a *Rāmabhakta,* a *Vitthalbhakta,* and so forth.

Bhakti. Literally, worship or adoration. It is the attitude of the *bhakta* towards God. It always implies a moral idea of sincerity and purity of worship, accompanied with love. Again and again the poet-saints affirm that there can be no *bhakti* without sincerity and love. *Bhakti* is, therefore, more than mere worship, which can be so easily a mere outward form. *Bhakti* must be the true feeling of the heart, of reverence, and love of God, whether expressed in outer forms of worship, or in the mental worship (*Mānas puja*).

Bhaktimārga. Bhakti-mārga, the way of *Bhakti.* Three ways are recognized for the deliverance of man from the succession of births and deaths, with their sins and sorrows, and with their good deeds and joys, as well. The *Dnyānamārga* [The Way of Knowledge] holds the highest place in the minds of philosophers, because, when by true Knowledge, Ignorance disappears, all causes of sin and sorrow disappear. The *Karma-mārga,* or Way of Works, is recognized by the poet-saints as a way, but a very hard way, and a very dangerous way. In the case of both, of the above ways the danger is pride, and with pride comes a fall. The safe way, the sure way, the easy way, for all high or low, is the *bhakti-mārga,* in which a man throws himself on the mercy of God, *bhakti* on man's part, and mercy, forgiveness, and salvation, on God's part. With *bhakti* sincere, and the consequent gift from God of *moksha* [salvation, deliverance], a return to this earth is avoided, and there is eternal life in the presence of God. Because it is a sure and easy way for all, the poet-saints give the *Bhakti-mārga* the highest preference. Although, the word etymologically does not imply it, the usage of the poet-saints in strongest terms emphasizes the moral side of *Bhakti,* not only sincerity in *Bhakti,* but a pure ethical life is essential to the very idea of *Bhakti.* Eknāth's writings are especially emphatic on this importance of internal and external moral purity.

Brahma. *Brahma* is the substance of which all things consist. Existing things have forms and names (*nāma* and *rupa*). That they exist and have *forms* and *names* is as real as is the real substance *Brahma.* To consider these forms, however, as different from *Brahma,* making a duality, is due to *ignorance,* that Ignorance personified is called *māyā.* (which see.)

Brahmachāri. A Brahman who observes the strictest chastity for a time or for life from a religious motive.

C

Chakōr. A bird that is said to subsist on moonbeams. This idea is very frequently used in poetic figures and illustrations.

Charitra. Actions, deeds, proceedings, exploits, history.

Chātaka. A bird said to drink only from the clouds, hence always eager for the rain. The idea is very frequently used in poetic figures and illustrations.

Chiplā. A musical instrument, consisting of two sticks rattled together.

Chūl. A fireplace. In its simplicity it may be three stones so arranged as to have the fire between them, and the pot or pan resting on them, or a semicircular erection of earth to contain the fire in its cavity, and support the cooking vessel on its rim.

D

Dakshiṇā. Money or presents given to Brahmans and others on special occasions.

Darshana. Literally, sight, seeing, looking. In the religous usage of the word there is, however, much more than the physical sight, seeing or looking. There is an implication of respect, reverence and worship. There is no English word corresponding with this use of *darśana.*

Dasarā. A festival commemorating the period of the year when the Marāthā Kings started out on their campaigns.

Dhotar. The garment worn by men, consisting of a long piece of cloth wound around the body, tucked in front at the waist and also behind taking the place of the European trousers.

Divāli. The annual festival of lights.

Dnyāna. 1. Knowledge in general. 2. Knowledge of a specific and religious kind.—that which is derived from meditation and the study of philosophy; which teaches man the divine origin and nature of his immaterial portion, and the unreality of corporal enjoyments, sufferings and experiences, and the illusoriness of the external and objective universe; and which sanctifying him during life from earthly attachments and fleshly affections, accomplishes for him after death emancipation from individual existence and reunion with the universal spirit. In some parts of India the word is pronounced *gyāna.*

Dnyānamārga. The Way of knowledge. (See Dnyāna).

G

Gāyatri. A sacred verse from the Vedas, repeated by Brahmans at their morning and evening devotions.

Ghatika. A period of twenty-four minutes.

Ghāṭ. 1 A mountainous range dividing countries. 2 A pass or difficult passage over a hill. 3 Quay, wharf, stairs, landing place (on banks of rivers or tanks). Hence applied by washermen, tanners, dyers, Brahmans, etc., to their respective places of resort.

Ghi. Clarified butter, also known as *tūp.* The butter is melted, thus removing the water that may be in it, and then preserved in jars.

Gotra. Family, race, lineage.

Guṇā. 1 A quality, attribute, affection, or property whether of matter or mind; a power, faculty, excellence, virtue; a property inherent or an affection supervenient in the most comprehensive sense. 2 The constitution of created things, as comprised in three *guṇas; satva* (existence, truth, goodness, brightness etc.) *raja* (energy, passion, action etc.,) *tama* (evil, darkness, ignorance etc.) All created things are a mixture of the three, *Satvaguṇa, Rajoguṇa,* and *Tamoguṇa,* and therefore, are spoken of as *Saguṇa* (possessing these *guṇas*), and Brahma, the *paramātmā* is *nirguṇa* (unpossessed by these qualities). In God, in good men, in good things the *satva* predominates. In evil men or spirits or demons the *tama* predominates. The *rajoguṇa* is in all as the activity of either the good or the evil, or both. In God all is *satva,* because it is the *satva* that is in activity (rajoguṇa). In man there is a mixture of the *satva* and *tama,* and the activity (rajoguṇa) makes man a mixture of good and evil, sometimes the good predominating, sometimes the evil.

Guru. A religious teacher; one who instructs in the Shāstras.

H

Harabarā. A vetch, gram. Cicer arientinum.

Haridās. Servants of Hari [Vishṇu]. Worshippers of Hari. Wandering singers who praise the deeds of Hari.

J

Japa. The repeating of *mantras* or the names of God. A rosary may be used so as to know the number of times the *mantra* or names have been used. As this outer form requires an inner reality, *japa* stands also for meditation, for worship, for prayer, indeed for the true spiritual life of a man. The correlative of *japa* is *tapa* (which see). *Tapa,* literally religious austerity, is also extended in meaning to comprise the outer religious life of a man. *Japa,* his inner religious life and *tapa* his outer religious life.

Jiva, Shiva. When *Jiva* and *Shiva* are thus used together *Jiva* stands for the individual *ātmā,* and *Shiva* for the Universal *ātmā.*

Jondhaḷā. A cereal plant or its grain. Hulcus sorghum.

K

Kaḍabā. The stalks with their leaves of the *jondhaḷā,* or *jvāri,* Hulcus sorghum, used for fodder.

Kailās. The Heaven of Shiva.

Kaliyuga. The present, fourth age of the world, the evil age. Its duration is considered to be 432,000 years, after which the world is to be destroyed. The present year A.D. 1926 corresponds with the *Kaliyuga* 5027. The initial year is 3101 B.C. The four *yugas* are the *Kritayuga, Tretāyuga, Dvāpārayuga* and the *Kaliyuga* The four *yugas* together make a *Mahāyuga* (Great *yuga,* 4,320,000 years. It is this evil *kaliyuga* that has necessitated the frequent *avatārs* to check evil and to save mankind from its effects.

Kalpa. A day of Brahma, 432 million years of mortals.

Karma. 1 An act or a deed. 2 Religious action, as sacrifice, ablution etc., 3 Destiny; destiny being only the allotment, to be enjoyed or suffered in the present life of the fruit of good and evil actions performed in former lives. 4 Deed or action. As all actions through the laws of cause and effect determine the actions in the next life. Karma is equivalent also to Fate.

Karmamārga. The law of works; the road to heaven through observance of rites and ceremonies and performance of virtuous deeds. (See *Dnyānamārga*, Way of Knowledge, and *Bhaktimārga,* Way of Devotion). The way of deeds. One of the three ways of Deliverance:—*Dnyānamārga, Karmamārga,* and *Bhaktimārga.*

Kathā. A Story, fable, exploits of Gods or heroes related with music and singing.

Kavaḍi. A cowrie. A shell used in making small change.

Kākiṇi. A weight of shells equal to 20 cowries.

Kāvaḍ. A bamboo lath provided with slings at each end in order to contain baskets, jars etc. and carried on the shoulder. Used for carrying water, vegetables etc.

Kirtan. Celebrating the praises of a god with music and singing. Reciting the names of the deity. In practice, however, it is a religious service of song. The leader has a topic which he delivers in song. He is accompanied with a chorus leader, and musical instruments. Following their leader the audience may break out in ecstatic repetitions of the names of God, or of the lines of a chorus.

Kshetra. A sacred spot, a sacred city, a place of pilgrimage.

Kulkarni. A village officer who keeps public records and keeps the accounts of cultivators in their relation to Government.

M

Mahant. 1. The chief or head of an order of Gosavis, Bairagis etc., a religious superior. 2 Applied to the head or leading man among paṇḍits, devotees etc.

Mahābhārata. The great epic relating to wars of the Pandavas and Kauravas, ascribed to Vyās as author.

Mahārāshtra. The great nation. The old name of the country occupied by the Marāthā people, now included in the Bombay Presidency.

Mana. Mind. According to Western psychology the mind is the soul itself viewed as thinking or imagining. Mana, however, is regarded as an organ [*indriya*] of thinking and imagining and not a part of the pure *Ātmā* (Soul).

Mandap. An open temporary structure, made with *bamboo* or other poles, with cloth roof and sides, erected for festal occasions, for marriages, *kirtans* etc.

Mantra. A text, prayer, hymn or verse, which possesses mystical or supernatural power.

Māyā. This word is usually translated "Illusion," but this is not a satisfactory translation. Vedantic philosophy postulates that there is but one substance, called *Brahma*, or *paramātmā*, or *ātmā*. This substance appears in the form of the universe, and to the various *forms* there are *names* [*nāma-rupa*]. These forms are temporary and changeable, and with the change of form the name disappears. It is due to Ignorance that these forms are supposed to be distinct from the One Substance. The reality of these forms is not denied, but that they are distinct from the One substance is denied. That they are distinct *i.e.*, that there is a duality, is the particular form of illusion which is indicated by the word *Māyā*. In usage Māyā becomes personified as the cause of the Ignorance (*adnyāna*) which sees duality where there is unity. One of the stock illustrations is that of gold in the form of various ornaments, each with its own name. That the gold appears in the form of various ornaments is not denied, but that those ornamental forms are permanent and distinct from the gold is denied. The ornaments can be melted; they disappear as ornaments, but the gold remains unchanged. To think the ornaments were distinct from the gold would be through Ignorance [*adnyāna*], and the cause of the ignorance, by a sort of personification is *māyā*.

Moḍi. Is the cursive writing of the Marāthi. The old Asoka alphabet of the inscriptions, 250 B.C., gradually developed in time into the *Devanāgari*, used in transcribing Sanskrit literature, as also Marāthi literature. In business writing however, haste being important, and the pen being lifted from the paper as little as possible, it led to a change in the form of the *Devanāgari* letters, which to the casual observer seem a different character, but which can be most easily traced back to the *Devanāgarị origin.* The tradition that Moḍi was brought from the south, or that it was the invention of Hemachandra in the 13th century, may be due to the character of the southern cursive writing, and it could well be that Hemachandra adopted it as the form for official documents. There is no doubt, however, that the *Modi* has developed from the *Devanāgari* simply by rapid writing, with the lifting of the pen from the paper as little as possible.

Moksha. Deliverance of the soul from the body, its exemption from further transmigration, with all its joys and sorrows, sins and good deeds, and its absorption into the divine essence.

Mukti. Exemption of the spirit from further migration and the reabsorption of it into its source, the divine monad, Brahma, the substratum and substance of universal being. This deliverance from births and deaths, must be understood to include in the idea the deliverance from the sins and sorrows, even from the good deeds and joys of life, for each life is made up of these. The four forms of *mukti* are *sāyujyatā, salokatā, samipatā* and *sarupatā,* (see sāyujyatā).

N

Namaskār. Worship, obeisance, reverential or respectful address or salutation. It is performed by joining the palms, inclining the head and pronouncing the word *namaskār. A sāshtāṅg namaskār* is the prostration on the ground, so that eight parts (*ashta*) of the body touch the ground, and is the most profound method of showing reverence to God or man.

Nirguṇ. Nir-guṇ, Literally without a quality. *Brahma*, or *ātmā, paramātmā* the one substance which appears to us as the universe, cannot be described in human words. It is indescribable (*avāchya*.) While the one substance cannot be described the forms in which it appears can be described, and their qualities determined. The forms with their names are, therefore, *saguṇ*, [*Sa-guṇ*] with quality, God, as a personal being creator of the special form, in which the universe appears, is recognized as one of the forms in which the One eternal substance appears. God, therefore, is *saguṇa*, that is, he has qualities which can be described in human understandable words. *Brahma* is *nirguṇ*; God (*iśvara*) is *saguṇ*. The gods, all *avatārs*, idols, and the visions of God, are all *saguṇa* manifestations of the *Nirguṇ Brahma*, or *nirguṇa ātmā*. The *Saguṇ Iśvara*, being but the one of the many forms in which the *Nirguṇ Iśvara* appears, are, of course, to be identified as the golden bracelet is identified with the gold of which it consists. The poet-saints therefore in their hymns of praise, their invocations, their worship, and their prayers, make no distinction. They are addressed as well to the *nirguṇ* God as to the *saguṇ*

God. This identity of the *saguṇ* and the *nirguṇ* is often asserted very definitely.

Nivṛitti. Cessation from worldly concerns and engagements; also Absorption into Brahma.

O

Ovi. A stanza of a particular metre of Marāthi verse.

P

Pada. A variety of metrical compositions, used in hymns or anthems. Very many of the poet-saints have written in this metre. (See the Padasangraha in the Kāvyasangraha Series for examples).

Pādukā. An impression of a foot on stone, worshipped as the trace of some god or guru.

Pānsupāri. A roll of the Piper-betel leaf with Areca nut, cloves, lime etc. (See *Viḍā*).

Pāp. Sin in the abstract, or an evil deed. It is the exact negative correlative of the word *puṇya*, goodness or holiness in the abstract, or a good or holy deed. That *pāp* and *puṇya*, evil and good deeds must receive a future reward of suffering or happiness is a part of Hindu philosophy, but this idea does not belong to the words themselves. Molesworth's Marāthi English Dictionary of 1831, founded on the Marāthi-Marāthi Dictionary of 1829, rightly defines these words. I differ absolutely from the Notes on these words in

Molesworth's Second Edition of 1857, and from its definition of the word *puṇya* as "merit," a meaning it never has had in Sanskrit, or in the whole course of Marāthi literature, until influenced by Molesworth's second edition. See further discussion under *puṇya.*

Peth. A region or large division of a city. A manufacturing or a trading town. A market town. A ward of a city.

Pradakshiṇā. Circumambulation of an object, keeping the right side towards it These objects may be idols, sacred trees, the *tulsi* plant, a temple, even a sacred city. Keeping the object to the left would imply irreverence.

Prahar. An eighth part of the day of 24 hours. A *prahar* is therefore a period of three hours. The prahars begin at sunrise, at six, hence Donprahar [*two-praharas*] is noon.

Prakriti. In philosophy *prakriti* and *purusha* are words that denote the material and the immaterial universe. *Prakriti* (Nature, matter phenomenon) conceived as female, and *Purusha* (male, the soul, life, activity) by their union make the whole universe, an anthropomorphic expression of the idea expressed in English as "matter and mind."

Prasād. 1 Favor, graciousness, propitiousness. 2 Any thing (a fruit, flower, rice etc.) given by an idol, a *guru*, a saint, as a blessing or a mark of favour." 3 Food etc. presented to an idol or a holy person to be distributed, thus honored, among worshippers etc. 4 The sweetmeats and fruit distributed among the audience at the conclusion of a *kathā, kirtan,* or puraṇic reading.

Prākrit. In the usage of the Marāthā poet-saints the *Prākrit* language means the Marāthi language. As distinguished from the Sanskrit (the polished language), it means the common vernacular of the people. As may be seen from the lives of the poet-saints and their works, they had to encounter a certain amount of opposition against their Marāthi, or *Prākrit* versions of the sacred Sanskrit texts. (See Eknāth's life, Bhaktalilāmrita Chapter 21).

Prārabdha. Deeds in former births determined the course of one's life in the birth previous to this. Deeds in the previous life have determined the course of one's present life. Deeds in the present life will determine the life in the next birth. This is the law of *prārabdha.*

Puṇya. Goodness or holiness in the abstract, or a good or holy deed. Its negative is *pāp,* or sin in the abstract, or an evil deed. In the definition of this word as also in the definition of the word pāp I differ absolutely from Molesworth's Marāthi and English Dictionary, second edition of 1857. In a note it says, "The word bears not the feeblest implication of holiness, godliness or purity of spirit." On the contrary it implies all three. And by its using the definition of "merit" (not found in the edition of 1831) an idea foreign to the word has since then been attached to this noble word. "Merit," meaning a future reward of a good deed, is no part of the meaning of the word *Puṇya*, which is simply goodness or holiness in the abstract or a holy or good deed. The idea of merit belongs to Indian philosophy, but not to the word *puṇya*. Every *puṇya* will have its reward in the future, as will every *pāp*, but this idea is not in the word itself.

The first edition of Molesworth of 1831, founded on the paṇdit's Marāthi-Marāthi edition of 1829 has the correct definition. See also Monier-Williams Sanskrit dictionary under *puṇya* and *pāp*. The word *puṇya*, twice used in the Ṛigveda, many times used in the Upanishads, and Bhagavadgitā, and all through old Marāthi literature, is the exact negative of *pāp*. It, in no single instance, means "merit" as implying a future reward.

Puranpoḷī. A wheaten cake with stuffing of coarse sugar, pea flour etc.

Purāṇ. A particular class of Hindu sacred literature, generally regarded as eighteen in number. They deal with stories of the creation of the world, its destruction, its renewal, of gods, goddesses, and heroes. The eighteen are Brahma, Padma, Vishṇu, Śiva, Liṅga, Garuḍa, Nārada, Bhāgavata, Agni, Skanda, Bhavishya, Brahmavaivarta, Mārkaṇḍeya, Vāmana, Varāha, Matsya, Kūrma and Vāyu, but there are other lists of 18, slightly varying from this. Of the Purāṇs the Bhāgavata, giving the life and teachings of Krishṇa, has had the greatest influence on the thought and life of the Marāthā poet-saints.

Purāṇik. "A Brahman well read in the Purāṇs. A public expounder of them." On account of the vast extent of Sanskrit literature, those who expound the sacred books have to specialize. There are those who make a speciality of expounding some Purāṇ and are known as Purāṇiks.

Purusha. See Prakriti.

R

Rāmāyaṇa. The great epic relating the exploits of Rām, ascribed to Vālmiki as author.

S

Sadguru. Literally a true, or good guru (see *Guru.*) While primarily the word applies to human teachers, or *gurus*, the poet-saints even applied it to God, for a *sadguru* is regarded as a manifestation of God. The Marāthā Poet-saints frequently refer to the high moral qualities, the sincerity, the unselfishness, the unhypocritical spirit, that marks a *sadguru,* as distinguished from a false guru.

Saguṇ. See Nirguṇ.

Samsāra. 1. The world, mundane existence, human life, man's mortal state. 2 The affairs of life; worldly business; the vocations and engagements, the cares and troubles of secularity.

Sannyāsi. One who has cast off all worldly possessions, and carnal or natural affections, an ascetic. The poet-saints distinguish between the hypocritical, formal *Sannyāsi*, who outwardly appears only to have given up all, and the true and sincere *sannyāsi*, whose giving up of the world is genuine.

Santa. A saint, practically synonymous with *sādhu* (which see). He is one who has lost worldly desires and devotes himself to the worship of God. But whatever he may appear outwardly, no one is a *santa* without purity of heart and life. The appellation *Kavi-santa*, or poet-saints, designate those saints who were poets. The Marāthā poet-saints begin with Dnyāneśvara, about A.D. 1290, so far as their works are known, and continue to the present day.

Satchidānanda. Existent-intelligence-joy. Although *Brahma*, or the *paramātmā* cannot be described in human words [*avāchya*], yet because, it is believed to *exist*, to be that which takes the form of *intelligent beings*, and to express itself in beings feeling *joy*—*Brahma* being the substrate of these—this definition of Brahma is very frequently employed. It should be noted that the two words, *existence*, intelligence and *joy* are not adjectives, but nouns. They do not connote that *Brahma* is *intelligent* and *happy*, but that the One existent substance, *Brahma* appears in the form of intelligent beings possessing joy and goodness.

Sādhana. The means employed to obtain deliverance from births and deaths and all that life implies in its sins and sorrows and even joys.

Sādhu. A holy man; a saint or sage; one of subdued passions and of contemplative habits. The poet-saints give the word a moral emphasis, hence a *sādhu* is a man of pure character, one truly devoted to God, a spiritually minded man; a good man. A man can appear hypocritically a *sādhu,* and not be a *sādhu,* for a *sādhu* must be pure in heart and life. The wandering professional *sādhu,* called such, may or may not be sincere, but he is not considered a true *sādhu* without purity of heart and life.

Sāshtāṅg-namaskār. See Namaskār.

Sāvadhāna. Literally attention, heed. At the moment of marriage, the priests in solemn tone repeat the words "*Sāvadhānam, sāvadhānam*" and at that moment the curtain between the bride and bridegroom is removed, and the marriage is complete.

Sāyujyata. The fourth of the four states in which *mukti* [final deliverance] is distinguished, *viz.*, absorption into the essence of Brahma. The four are *Sayujyatā* [absorption into the essence of Brahma;] *Salokatā* [residence in the heaven of a particular deity]; *Samipatā* [Nearness to the Deity]; and *Sarupatā* [Bearing the likeness of God].

Shānti. Peace. Unruffled mind.

Shloka. A verse, a stanza, a quantity of four lines. A particular metre; praise. In the Marāthi commentaries the *Shloka* commented on is the Sanskrit text.

Shrāddha. A kind of funeral rite or ceremony in honour of the departed spirits of dead relatives, observed with great strictness at various fixed periods, especial honor being given to paternal and maternal ancestors.

Shudra The fourth grand division of the Hindu body; also an individual of it. The four grand divisions are *Brahmaṇ,* [the priestly caste]; *Kshatriya,* [the warrior, military, governing class]; *Vaishya* [agricultural and mercantile class]and *Shudra* [the servile class, whose duty is to serve the upper three]. The *atishudra,* also called *anāmik, antyaja,* are those still lower than the shudra, and outside of the four grand divisions. Hence they are *asprishya* [Untouchable] or *anāmika* [Unmentionable].

Shruṭi. The Vedas severally or collectively. The word is from the Sanskrit, meaning "hearing."

Siddhi. A supernatural power or faculty supposed to be acquirable through the performance of certain magical, mystical, or alchemical rites or processes. Eight are enumerated, *viz., aṇimā, mahimā, garimā, laghimā, prāpti, prakāmya, ishitva,* and *vaśitva.* The powers or *siddhis* are personified as female beings, or *siddhis,* who come and serve those who by their austerities or otherwise gain those powers.

Skandha. A section of a book, a book, a chapter.

Stotra. 1 Praise, panegyric, eulogium. 2 A book or writing in celebration of the praises of God; also a hymn.

Svāmi. A master or lord, the master or lord of, also the proprietor or owner of. Applied to the Deity, a god, a king, or prince, a spiritual preceptor, a husband, a holy personage, a learned Brāhmaṇ, a *Gosavi, Sannyāsi* etc. It is used also as a title, as Keśava-svāmi.

T

Tapa. Religious austerity, pious mortification of the body. It is especially connected with the *yoga* system, and the *yogis* carry it to its extreme limit. But it also has less austere usage, meaning the duties of life, the special duties of Brahmans, Kshatriyas, Vaishyas and Shudras. It is, therefore, the correlative of *Japa. Japa* signifying the inner spiritual life, and *tapa* the outer religious life. (See Japa).

Tilak. The spot or line made with coloured earths or unguents upon the forehead. It is considered either as an ornament or as a sectarial distinction.

Tirtha. 1 A holy or sacred place, any place of pilgrimage, but especially particular spots along the course of sacred streams or in the vicinity of sacred springs. 2 A holy stream, or water brought from one. Water in which a Brahman, *sannyāsi* etc., has dipped his feet, or which has been poured over an idol; holy water.

Tulsi. A plant venerated by the Hindus, Holy Basil, Ocymum sanctum. It is usually grown in an earthen altar before the door of the house, or in the garden behind the house. Its leaf is used in offerings, in garlands, and its stalks also have sacred uses. Those worshipping the plant go around it, keeping it to the right [*pradakshiṇā*] with palm to palm, repeating a *mantra,* or prayer.

U

Upanishad. The oldest philosophical literature.
Upāsanā. Worship or religious service.

V

Vaikuṇṭha. The Heaven of Vishṇu.

Vastu. The real as opposed to the unreal. Brahma. The Universal *Ātmā. Substance.* The substance of which the Universe consists, namely Brahma.

Vairāgi. An ascetic or devotee; one who has subdued his worldly desires and passions. The word is also applied to a class of religious mendicants. The word is also pronounced *bairāgi.* The poet-saints distinguish between the true and the hypocritical *vairāgi.*

Vairāgya. 1 Indifference to or absence of worldly desires or passions. 2 Popularly, Renunciation of all sensuous delights or gratification.

Vedas. The oldest of the Indian Scriptures. The four Vedas are, the Rigveda, the Yajurveda, the Sāmaveda, and the Atharvaveda.

Viḍā. A roll of the leaf of Piper-betel with Areca-nut, cloves, lime etc. It is usually chewed after a meal. It is distributed to an audience after a *kirtan,* or any public assembly, and is the final act. It is believed to be a digestive, and also as purifying the mouth. It is generally called *pan-supāri* [leaf-supāri nut]. Many have the habit of chewing it constantly.

Videhi. Literally, one without a body [*vi-deha*]. In usage however, it implies a temporary or permanent absorption of the mind in a way to make one unconscious of the possession of a body, as when one is intensely listening to a *kirtan,* he is for the time being a *videhi.* Or when through a life of constant contemplation of the *ātmā,* or of God, the ascetic or devotee loses all thought of his body, of cold or heat, hunger or thirst, desires or passions, he is a *videhi.* A man is a *videhi* when the spiritual completely dominates the physical.

Viveka. Right-thinking. To the Vedantist right-thinking is the discrimination between reality and unreality.

W

Waḍā. 1 A stately or large edifice, a mansion or palace. 2 A division of a town, a quarter, a ward, as Brahmanwāḍā, Mahārwāḍā. 3 An enclosed piece of meadow-field, or garden ground; an enclosure. 4 A cluster of huts of agriculturists, a hamlet.

Y

Yama. The god who rules over the spirits of the dead.

Yoga. Spiritual or abstract devotion; union with Brahma through abstract meditation, or contemplation; also the practice or exercise of this sort of worship.

Yogabhrashṭa. One who was interrupted in his preceding birth during the performance of *Yoga* [abstract meditation upon *Brahma*]. As an example, a pious outcaste, devoted to Eknāth, is called a *Yogabhrashta.* In the Autobiography of Bahiṇābāi, a calf, because of its peculiar pious actions, is called a *yogabhrashṭa.* Indeed any pious person can be described as a *yogabhrashṭa,* as one whose pious life in a former birth was accidentally interrupted and has now a further opportunity.

Yogi. 1 A performer of the abstract meditation called *yoga.* 2 An ascetic or devotee in general. Popularly a *yogi* is supposed to be able to gain extraordinary powers through his practice of *yoga,* called *siddhis* (which see), and the ash-covered *yogi* is able to instil much fear in the minds of the ignorant. The poet-saints, of course, distinguish between the hypocritical *yogi* and the true *yogi* whose heart and life must be pure.

Yojana. A measure of distance equal to four *Kos* roughly about eight miles.

APPENDIX II

NOTES ON THE BHIKSHUGITA.

The Bhikshugita of Eknāth is a commentary on the Eleventh *skandha* and 23rd chapter of the Bhagāvata Purāṇa, which chapter is also known as the Bhikshugita.

A. ORIGINAL SOURCES OF INFORMATION REGARDING EKNĀTH.

The oldest account giving a full history of Eknāth, is by Keśavasvāmi, written probably sometime previous to 1684. This account by Keśavasvāmi was very closely followed by Mahipati, in his Bhaktalilāmrita, completed in 1774. Twelve years previous to this, in 1762, Mahipati had completed his Bhaktavijaya, in which chapters 45 and 46 are devoted to the life of Eknāth. This Bhaktavijaya account of Eknāth was based, at least in part, on a document or documents other than those used by Keśavasvāmi, and followed by the Bhaktalilāmṛita. It differs from Keśavasavāmi's account in some very important and significant details, besides being very incomplete. The life of Eknāth, as popularly known, is taken from the Bhaktalilāmṛita, Chapters 13 to 24.

Aside from the above there are frequent very brief references in Eknath's own works to his Grandfather Bhānudās, and the pious line from which he was descended. (See Poet-Saints of Mahārāshṭra Series No. 1 on Bhānudās). Eknāth's Grandson, Mukteśvara, has ascribed to him a chapter in Eknāth's life called the Śri Khaṇḍyākhyāna. And finally Bhimasvāmi Shirgāvkar, about 1797, wrote a short account of Eknāth in which he seems to follow the Bhaktavijaya account rather than that of the Bhaktalilāmṛita. Because of the impression Eknāth made on his generation, very many poets since his day have sung his praises, but have not added any details regarding his life. (For a translation of the Bhaktalilāmṛita account of Eknāth see *The Poet-Saints of Mahārāshṭra Series No.* 2)

B. THE LIFE OF EKNĀTH

(*A Resumé of Bhaktalilamṛita Chapters* 13—24)

1. THE ANCESTRY OF EKNĀTH

The Great Grandfather of Eknāth was Bhānudās. (See Bhaktavijaya chapters 42 and 43 translated in *The Poet-Saints of Mahārāshṭra Series No.* 1.) Very early inclined to the religious life, he unwillingly followed for a time the life of a peddler of cloth. His strict honesty, and his system of fixed prices, brought him success, but his heart was on the religious life and he cast aside his money making business, and devoted the rest of his life to that of an ascetic.

Eknāth's Grandfather Chakrapāṇi and his father Suryanārāyaṇa, and mother Rukmiṇi, were noted for their piety and their nobleness of character. The Bhaktalilāmṛita account and the Bhaktavijaya account differ as to who cared for Eknāth during his boyhood. The Bhaktavijaya says he was cared for by his parents, but the Bhaktalilāmṛita asserts that the parents died early, and the care of Eknāth fell to the grandparents.

2. THE BOYHOOD OF EKNĀTH.

Eknāth was born at Paiṭhaṇ, known also by its ancient name of Pratishṭhāna, a sacred city, in the Hyderabad State, on the Godāvari river. Marathi Scholars have differed as to dates, some like Mr. Pāngārkar give his birth as 1528 and death as 1599, but Mr. Bhave and others, birth 1548 and death 1609.

Eknāth very early showed an inclination to the religious life. Even in his play he showed that his mind was on God-worship, and pious thought. Feeling the need of a *guru* to show him the way, and hearing a heavenly voice directing him to one Janārdan at Devagiri, the modern Daulatabad, he started at once without even asking the permission of his grandparents. Janārdan recognized his sincere desire for knowledge, and admitted him as his disciple. Eknāth showed extraordinary devotion to his *guru,* and gained his *guru's* respect, and love. Three miraculous stories are told of him during this period of discipleship; his assuming the form of Janārdan, the manifestation of Dattātreya, and Eknāth's vision of God on Mount Sulabha.

3. JANĀRDAN AND EKNĀTH GO ON A PILGRIMAGE.

Janārdan took Eknāth with him on a short pilgrimage. On the way they fell in with one Chandrabhat, who joined the party. Urged by Janārdan, Eknāth begins his literary career by producing a Marathi version of a section of the Bhāgavata Purāṇa, under the title, Chatushloki Bhāgavata. Chandrabhat returned with them to Devagiri, and at his request was, with due ceremony, buried alive.

4. EKNĀTH IS NOW SENT ON A LONG PILGRIMAGE.

Saying an affectionate farewell to Janārdan, Eknāth begins a pilgrimage, intended to cover even the most distant parts of India. He first goes to the sacred shrines in the North. On his return, with the intention of visiting the southern shrines, he passes through his home town, Pratishṭhāna.

During all this period of discipleship and pilgrimage, his grandparents were plunged into the deepest sorrow, not knowing what had become of him. They finally were successful in learning of his relations with Janārdan. The aged couple visit Janārdan, and are comforted by his assurances of their grandson's welfare. They, however, persuade Janārdan that they need their grandson, and obtained from him a letter to Eknāth telling him to remain at Pratishṭhāna. When, therefore, the parents recognized him as he was passing through their town, the letter was presented, and Eknāth bowed to the command of his *Guru.*

5. EKNĀTH'S MARRIAGE AND HOME LIFE.

Knowing Eknāth's indifference to the worldly life, the grandparents appealed again to Janārdan and obtained a written command to Eknāth to settle down to a married life, which he called the most honorable of all modes of life. A worthy bride was found, and after extensive preparations, and with many guests, the wedding ceremony was performed. Girjābāi, proved a true helpmeet, and joined with him in his religious acts, and in his remarkable philanthropic spirit, and acts of mercy. Soon after his marriage he had the sorrow of losing his Grandparents and his beloved *guru,* Janārdan.

6. STORIES OF EKNĀTH'S EVENTFUL LIFE.

How a merchant to whom he owed money was miraculously paid; how God in the guise of a Brahman came to serve him; his readings of the Bhāgavata; Brahman envy; his hospitality to four Brahman chance guests, and to three Muhammadans; Brahman hostility; Eknāth stays the death of Krishṇadās until he finishes his version of the Rāmāyaṇa, and he aids in the marriage ceremony of the idol Pāndurang with that of Rukmiṇi.

7. HIS PILGRIMAGE TO PAṆḌHARPUR.

His long desire to visit Paṇḍharpur is finally realized. He and a large company with him, singing the praises of God on the way, arrive at Paṇḍharpur. *Kirtans* and worship are performed with intense enthusiasm. The assembled *bhaktas* wish to hear from Eknāth's own lips the story of how his Grandfather Bhānudās brought back the image of Vithobā, which had been taken away to Vidyānagara by the king. He tells the story of Bhānudās and of his marvellous deliverance from an expected cruel death. Eknāth's return to his home was an occasion for enthusiastic welcome.

8. OTHER EVENTS IN EKNĀTH'S LIFE.

Shripād, a great *sannyāsi* appears, whose strange actions excite both respect and ridicule. He brings a dead donkey to life, and those envious Brahmans, who were opposed to Eknāth, use this *sannyāsi* as an opportunity to show their spite against Eknāth. At Shripād's own request Eknāth buries him alive. Eknāth's Brahman enemies accuse him of an unlawful act, and threaten excommunication, unless he performs a miracle to prove that his act was a lawful one. The miracle of the stone bull eating from his hand proved his innocence. Other disbelieving Brahmans, who had not seen the miracle demand another, and the stone bull leaping into the river answers their doubts.

9. EKNĀTH GOES TO ALANDI.

Eknāth had deep reverence for the poet-saint Dnyāneśvara, and with a large company went to visit his shrine at Aḷandi. The town was a deserted one at that time, and the pious pilgrims, unable to obtain food, were miraculously fed by God, who in the form of shopkeeper supplied all with the materials of their food, without charge. Warned in a dream that the root of a tree was pressing on the neck of Dnyāneśvara in his tomb, Eknāth opened the tomb and pushed the root aside. The company of pilgrims then returned.

Eknāth was a student of Dnyaneśvara's great commentary on the Bhagavadgitā. The copy he possessed had many copyist's errors. He is said to have corrected them, and gave many public readings from the work.

10. RĀṆYĀ MAHAR AND HIS WIFE.

Among the enthusiastic listeners at Eknāth's *Kirtans*, were even outcastes, for all pious souls were welcomed by him. Rāṇyā and his wife, Unmentionables as they were called, learned from Eknāth's lips that all were equal before God, and because they wished to have Eknāth's blessing, invited him to dine with them. He accepted the invitation. The Brahmans were furious, and lay in wait to catch him in the deed. Rāṇyā's wife made careful preparations, and when ready, awaited Eknāth's arrival. He came, or was it God who assumed his form? For the Brahman spies, rushing back and forth between Eknāth's home and the hut of Rāṇyā, the Unmentionable, saw Eknāth in both places, in one, dining at his own home, in the other, being lovingly ministered to by Rāṇyā Mahār and his wife.

11. EKNĀTH'S DAILY LIFE.

Envious Brahmans, who saw their gains lessened by Eknāth's popularity, were constantly working against him. His miraculous deeds they ascribed to the power of demons. He pursued, however, his even course of life, which included his regular morning devotions, his readings from the Bhāgavata and other sacred books, and his evening *kirtans,* that extended far into the night.

Among the miraculous stories related are those of his returning to a man a touchstone that had been left in his care. And God comes in the form of a Brahman, called Khaṇdyā, and serves hm without compensation, as a menial.

12. EKNĀTH'S FORGIVING SPIRIT AND DEEDS OF MERCY.

Four thieves listen to his *kirtan,* and then hide in his house until all are asleep. But while seeking for what they could steal, they suddenly become blind. Just then they find themselves in Eknāth's presence in the Godroom. They confess their evil intention, their sight is restored, Eknāth forgives them, and they leave converted to a good life.

A poor Mahār thief, emaciated by cruel treatment in prison, escapes and crawls to Eknāth's door, where a *kirtan* was going on. He hides, but when all were gone, Eknāth spies him, and pities his condition. Girjābāi, aroused from her sleep, cooks some simple food, and Eknāth feeds the Mahār with his own hands, covers him with a blanket, and thus saves his life, and obtains a pardon for him. The Brahmans find fault with Eknāth for this deed of mercy, but he is undeterred in his kindness to all. A Brahman Ghost is delivered from his curse by the touch of Eknāth's hand, because of his kind deed to the Mahār thief.

13. EKNĀTH'S LITERARY ACTIVITIES.

Beginning with the Chatushloki Bhāgavata, Eknāth's literary activities were largely in the form of commentaries, and short philosophic works, and Abhangs. His first large work was the commentary on the eleventh *skandha* of the Bhāgavata Purāṇa, known as the Eknāthi Bhāgavata.

14. EKNĀTH'S BHĀGAVATA BRINGS HIM PERSECUTION.

There were those who strongly opposed Marathi versions of the sacred Sanskrit texts, and Eknāth's attempts to make the sacred books accessible to those who were unacquainted with Sanskrit brought him persecution. A Brahman copied the first two chapters of Eknāth's Bhāgavata, and took them with him to Benares. Sitting by the river bank he read aloud from its pages. The very orthodox disciples of the chief *Sannyāsi* complained to their head of this desecration of the holy book. The Brahman was summoned. Examination proved him innocent of composing the Marathi version. Eknāth, being the guilty person, two disciples were sent to Pratisṭhāna to summon him to appear before the *Sannyāsi*, and answer to the charge. Eknāth acquiesced, and made the long journey to Benares. Eknāth, without any formal trial, was condemned by the *Sannyāsi* to be beaten, five blows by each of his three hundred disciples. The disciples, however, less revengeful than their head, were cautious, and as each one looked at Eknāth he seemed in the form of an *avatār* of God. And the *Sannyāsi* himself, became converted, and helped him to finish the remaining chapters of the version. The orthodox Brahmans of Benares were, however, not satisfied. They took his manuscript and threw it into the river, but the Bhāgirathi river, in the form of a jewelled Goddess, put out her hands and saved the book. The Brahmans now wished to worship Eknāth. He refused such worship for himself, but arranged for their worship of the Book.

While returning to Pratishṭhāna Eknāth met the ascetic Dāsopant Digambar*, whom he had long wished to meet. Eknāth had a hearty welcome on his return to his home, and soon after he celebrated with great eclat the birthday of Krishṇa.

15. EKNĀTH'S FORGIVING SPIRIT AND KINDNESS.

Eknāth's humble, forgiving and kindly spirit are illustrated by several stories. His forgiveness of a Muhammadan who spat on him led to the Muhammadan's conversion. He saw a little Mahār boy in pain on the burning sand of the river, and carried him on his shoulder

*See Journal of the American Oriental Society Vol. 42, pages 251—279. "*The Maratha Poet-Saint Dāsopant Digambar*", by Justin E. Abbott.

to his mother. A Brahman leper comes to Eknāth to be cleansed, and pleads that that good deed of his kindness to the Mahār boy, if transferred to him would cure him. Eknāth took some water and poured it on the leper's hand. The leprosy vanished, and the Brahman regained his beautiful form. Eknāth, loved and honored by the pious men and women who flocked to his *kirtans,* could not, however, escape the envy of some. They showed this in the case of the Goddess of the river, who assuming the form of a beautiful woman, came to listen to Eknāth's readings of the Purāṇa. When these evil minded men saw her vanish in the river they were converted, and confessed to him their fault. Eknāth's gentleness and tact led to the conversion of an impious merchant.

16. EKNĀTH'S SON HARI.

To Eknāth and Girjābāi were born a son and two daughters. The daughters were in time given in happy marriage. The son, Hari, was given every educational advantage, and he became learned in Sanskrit, but proud of his knowledge. He became ashamed of his good father, who gave *kirtans* in the language of the common people. He left his father's home and went to Benares to be among the learned Sanskrit *pandits.* But Eknāth was now getting old, and he had a strong longing to have his son return. He went to Benares to persuade him to return. Hari assented on two conditions, that the father should give up giving *kirtans* in Marathi, and that he should not eat food prepared by others outside of his home. Eknāth accepted, and the two returned. Hari now performed the *kirtans* in Sanskrit, but the crowds that used to come, and were understandingly led by Eknāth in enthusiastic worship, no longer appeared. Those who came could not understand, and got up and left. No longer at the reading of the Purāṇas did the *wāḍi* swarm with men and women.

But a miracle, that took place in the home of a pious woman led to Hari's conversion. Eknāth again resumed his *kirtans,* the old devoted crowd returned, clapping their hands, and listening with the old time enthusiasm.

17. EKNĀTH CARES FOR AN IDIOT BOY GAVĀBĀ.

A mother did not know what to do with her idiot boy. She heard of Eknāth, and from her humble village she brought the boy and placed him at Eknāth's feet. The kindly Eknāth received the boy, and tactfully, and sympathetically helped him in heart and intellect, until the supposed idiot, developed in mind and heart, became the poet to whom Eknāth entrusted the completion of the Rāmāyaṇa, on which he was working as the hour of his death approached.

18. EKNĀTH'S FINAL HOURS.

Eknāth, now an old man and infirm, felt that the time of his departure was at hand, and announced this to his sorrowing friends. Some envious to the very last, expressed their feelings in remarking that after all Eknāth would die as did other men, and be carried on the shoulders of men to the burning place. The pious, who loved Eknāth, expressed the wish that he should die in some special way. Eknāth assented, and weak as he was, arose from his bed, bathed, changed his clothes, took his *viṇā* in his hand, and repeating God's names aloud, went down to the river, accompanied with a sorrowing, weeping crowd. Inspired by the occasion, Eknāth sang praises to God, and then saying his loving farewell, waded into the water up to his waist. Calling loudly on the name of God, his soul left its abode, and from above, the gods, who were watching the solemn scene, showered flowers.

19. THE MIRACULOUS ASHVATTHA TREE

The next day when his son and friends came to gather up Eknāth's ashes, a surprise met their eyes. A fresh Tulsi plant and a small Ashvattha tree, with tender, brilliant leaves, were growing in the ashes. "It is Eknāth himself, manifesting himself in this Ashvattha tree," they exclaimed. And they built a stone platform around it, to preserve it. And on the platform they placed Eknāth's *pādukā,* so that it might be the sacred place where the pious might come, worship and realize the desires of their hearts.

C. THE BHIKSHUGITA

1. THE BHĀGAVATA PURĀṆA

Among the 18 Purāṇas, the one most used and honored by the Maratha Poet-Saints is the Bhāgavata Purāṇa. Scholars have not yet come to an agreement as to the date of its composition. There is strong evidence that it could not have been written later than 900 A.D. As to how much earlier it may have been written there is no unanimity of opinion. Any one familiar with the Bhāgvata Purāṇ and with the writings of Dnāyeshvara, the first in the known list of Maratha Poet-saints, will have evidence that he was deeply influenced by the Bhāgavata Purāṇa, which in its turn was influenced by the Bhagavadgitā*. Eknāth also was profoundly influenced by the Bhāgavata Purāṇa. Of his writings the Chatushloki Bhāgavata is a commentary on the ninth chapter of the second *skandha* of the Bhāgavata Purāṇa. The Shukāshṭaka is a commentary on eight *shlokas* from the Bhāgavata Purāṇa. The Eknāthi Bhāgavata is a commentary on the eleventh *skandha* of the Bhāgavata Purāṇa.

2. THE BHIKSHUGITA OF THE BHĀGAVATA PURĀṆA.

The twentythird chapter of the eleventh *skandh* of the Bhāgavata Purāṇa is also known as the Bhikshugita, The Mendicant's Song. It is somewhat in the nature of a parable, told by Krishṇa to Uddhava. Uddhava had expres-

---

*See my note on the word for word quotations in the Bhāgavata Purāṇa taken from the Bhagavadgitā, Indian Antiquary Vol. XXI page 94.

sed a doubt whether it were possible for a man to keep his mind in perfect peace [*śānti*] under insults and persecutions. Krishṇa assures him that it is possible, and relates the story of a miser who lived only for wealth. Losing it, however, and reduced to direst poverty, he repents and becomes a *sannyāsi.* His conversion is disbelieved, and insults and persecution follow. Through it all, however, the converted miser preserves perfect peace of mind. This story is told in the Sanskrit text of the Bhāgavata Purāṇa is 62 verses.

3. THE BHIKSHUGITA OF EKNĀTH

Eknāth in his commentary on this chapter of the Bhāgavta Purāṇa expands the 62 verses of the Sanskrit text into 1004 Marathi verses. He does this by describing in fuller detail the life of the miser, his methods of gaining wealth, his penuriousness, his eventual loss of all, his disgrace, his dire poverty, and then his conversion, followed by insults and persecution, in which his perfect peace of mind is preserved. Eknāth also has in this chapter very fully developed his thoughts on the evil results of the lust for wealth, on how to rightly use wealth, and how through a sincere approach to God the heart can become pure. "Bhakti is to be considered pure only when there is in it the love of God."